Dr. R___ ___ ___/__/__
We love
already s_
But you're a w___ __ I appreciate
~~caring~~ person. every thing about her
wonderful care. here.

The Hills Where the Black Spruce Grow

Picture on the back cover
Gail, myself, and 6 of soon
to be 11 grandchildren.
They love and hope their Gigi
recovers!

Dale M. Johnson

Dale M. Johnson

Copyright © 2016 by Dale M. Johnson
All Rights Reserved

No part of this book may be reproduced, stored in a retrieval system, or transmitted by any means without the written permission of the author.

ISBN 9781495919725

First Printing 2016
Printed in the United States of America

*Dedicated
to my wife and dear friend, Gail
and my three wonderful children
Eric, Amy, and Alex.*

CONTENTS

Introduction: xii
On the Hills Where the Black Spruce Grow 1
The Rocks that Lifted Us Up 5
The Girl that Got the Pig's Ear 9
Ice Fishing My Way 15
The Horse That Got Away 19
Some Sheep Stories 25
Raising Geese and Turkeys 30
The Boar Got Hammered 35
Indian Trees and Great Grandma's Stories 40
Tractors Can Fly 45
Yumping Yimminy 52
Sox Saves Some Sheep 55
Perspectives 58
Mushroom Hunting and Looking at Life 62
Bob and Opal 65
Buster Goes Mad 69
John Deere Hit in the Rear 72
The Corn Got Buried 75
Chicken Feathers 79
Oh- Rats! 82
The Bull that Nearly Got Me 85

Old School Bike Riding	93
Hay Stories	97
Beaver Dam Things	100
Fruits and the Human Spirit	103
Squirrel Hunting	107
Harvest Time	110
An Afternoon to Remember	113
Tractor on the Edge	116
Grandma's Visit Rules	119
Thanksgiving Thoughts	124
The Winter Fun and the Wild Toboggan Ride	126
Tomatoes and the Large Family Ways	130
Fox Trapping in Days Gone By	134
Snowshoe Rabbit Hunting	137
Gift from the Indians	141
Volunteering in Belize	144
Time Warped	147
What's Better than Fun?	150
Spring Things	153
Kites, Rain, and Flowers in the Woods	155
Lists, Mottos, and Goals for Life	157
Getting Ready for the Fair	160
The Wild Dog Pack	163
A Trip Down Memory Lane and the 21st Century	166

Finding Your Voice and Other Things	169
The Bear Facts and Wild Animals	173
Class Reunions and How We Become Who We Are	176
Following God's Will and the Deer Crash	178
Fall and the Seasons of Life	182
Being Thankful in a Troubled World and Time	184
Retirement Watches	186
The Root Cellars and Fall Stuff	190
Should've	194
Thanksgiving is for Each Us	196
Dorothy Goes Home	198
Proud Father Welcomes new Daughter-In-Law	200
The Layton Rocking Chair	202
The Teacher's Request for His Students	205
The Wintery Day	206
Beaver Pond Evening	207
Christmastime Rhyme	208
The Hungry Pond	209
Ice Fishing - The Hole Hopping Method	216
Our Florida Trip	220
Reflection Season	223
A White Bird in the Flock	225
Let it Snow	226
The Man from the Woods	228

Quaking Aspen and Whispering Pines 232
The Blue Memory Fire 234
A Special Note: 237

Introduction:

During my thirty years of teaching both my students and my own children often asked to hear stories that I would tell. I am pretty good at remembering these tales, trials, and tragedies of days gone by. As the years progress, I wonder if this gift will fade away, like my ability to play sports has already done.

Additionally, a couple of drunk drivers have hit me, the last one being a head-on collision. I also rammed my head into a garage wall. This accident was a bleak reminder of a saying that my grandmother Lida was fond of, "It's always later than you think!" The crash temporally paralyzed me on the left half of my body, albeit short-lived, praise God. The lingering effect being a constant pain in the neck- a condition that I am occasionally believed to cause for others.

Life as a youth on traditional livestock and crop farm life was certainly no picnic, hard, hot, and dirty work, without much fun, was the order of the day. Pitching manure, picking rocks, hauling hay, driving tractors, weeding gardens, making firewood, cleaning house, and doing dirty dishes were my most vivid memories. Life in those days was not a lot of laughs. My wife has tried to tell me that this was not uncommon for kids in rural communities. That may be true although I have my doubts about this. I guess I was farmer boy of the 50s and 60s similar to the harsh life mentioned in the stories written by Laura Ingalls Wilder.

The other side of life involved spending time at my grandma's house and cottage on a nice lake. She was the classic: a great cook, crafty card player, super seamstress, excellent fisherman, and a kind soul. I always thought I was the luckiest boy alive when I was with her.

My grandmother had something special and wonderful in her life. Only now do I realize what it was – time. She didn't spend her time watching DISH Network, taking cell phone calls, surfing the net, or rushing around to make various appointments. Her life was hers to enjoy, spending precious moments alone in turn with each of her seven grandchildren was one of her greatest delights. When my turn came around it was a treasure to glory in. Making homemade beef stew, soft sugar cookies with raisins, and being able to go into the milk delivery truck and choose a bottle of buttermilk or chocolate milk sure was cool. I loved my grandmother, and she loved me. It was simple as that.

All those many years now since her death in 1981, yet those happy memories can still pull me out of the doldrums. I pray that one day at least one person can say that about me. At this point, I have six grandchildren and pray I have inherited some of her kindness magic.

Yes, times were different, life seemed slower although you were required to do a lot more physical labor in those days. A person had to dig up their potatoes to keep them from becoming a couch potato. I still do my own vegetable garden.

These are the stories of days gone by on a southern Michigan farm where the challenges were big and the times left for fun seemed small. The lessons of life come from all directions like the winds of life some favorable and some ill. Then we never knew what the day, week, or month held in store.

As a middle child with an older brother and younger brother, I believed that I got a rough row to hoe, more than my fair share. Research dealing with birth order shows most of us middles believe that to be the case. I also had an older sister. She lived a somewhat different life than us boys – being a first and only girl gives you different results. The lessons learned have lasted well.

First, work as hard and fast as you safely can while remembering the old adage "haste makes waste."

Second, things can and often do go wrong especially on a farm. The Bible tells us that when we are given trials, we can become bitter or better. The latter is more likely to help make you be the person you pray you might become – with God's help.

Last, a determined person can often outlast or out-think most people who think they are smarter than you with time and persistence. I hope these true stories are memorable and fun. Enjoy the many trips down the farm lane and have a cup of warm cheer on me.

On the Hills Where the Black Spruce Grow

If only the mighty oak would tell tales of matters thereabouts. The giant tree once stood proud and grand. Like it had for at least 175 years or so. Changing times have pointed long and hard toward the demise of our family's farm. All old, small farms are waning. Our farm had been in business since Michigan became a state in 1837. No one anywhere in the Great Lakes State could have beat that record. Now all is gone, all 300 acres sold, the pages of time turn steadily. American Indians that left just before us left few hints of their existence. A few burial mounds of their past remain in places I shall never name. Are our present times better now – I dare say not! The world struggles and a culture of drugs, alcohol, and a lack of self-discipline are increasing rapidly. Often I worry that America and its once great middle class are all but gone. The rich number now in the millions and the poor service-workers are growing in number. I wonder what is to become of us in the shrinking middle class. I see no hope of the six-digit club for me. So enough of this nonsense on with the stories that you may relate to in many ways. I venture to say some may jostle your memories more than you care to remember. Some will make you reminisce and the rest please just follow along. I hope to draw a smile, bring a grin and at least an, oh darn. Will you remember the wrenching days of farm life? Most all-work-and-little-play was there for me. Now about the author, who really cares. The normal stuff, M.S.U. Land-grant University graduate, farm boy, and retired teacher. Along the way salesman, banker, counselor, advisor, coach, parent, husband, father, uncle, etc.... You've got the picture. I was hoping you all would make me rich so I can give most of my fortune away to those that have not been as blessed as I have been. I am a very grateful man, and I have been saved by God's grace in ways I could never have earned or deserved.

Most of us believe we have something to say and a story to share. As I grow older, the swinging pendulum of time is telling me to record a few of my thoughts. It's best to pass on my experience to future generations. I have lived somewhat a trying life but does that not harden you for the trials that we all face in the paths of our lives.

Most of my youth was not much fun. A large amount of very difficult physical labor and even fewer rewards. My parents forced my brothers and sister to be the workers; my parents were the tough bosses probably not that uncommon.

Have you ever picked rocks, pitched manure, hauled hay, and weeded the garden or driven tractor all day all summer in the hot sun with no breaks? That was my entire life until I was 23 years old. I never had even one vacation at a beach - that was not in the cards for me. I started at age 7. My wife says it was common in my time 1957-1973. She may have a good point, but she never lived that hard way of life. Oh, I had a savior, my grandma, Lida. She was my relief from my plight and rescued me whenever she could. Thank God and bless her kind and wonderful soul.

You all know her in spirit best cookie maker on earth, best cook in the countryside, and she even bought you a treat from the milkman, sometimes chocolate milk. That sure dates me – glass bottles, home delivery, and even glass bottles at school. My older brother and sister really did walk to school in the winter. I did too, but only one fall for half a year. A mile by road much less across the fields. We usually took the later. It really was cold at our three-room school; we wore coats, boots, and even gloves in the classroom in cold weather. Our milk would actually ice up at times out in the hallway, as it was very cold because there was no heat at all. Then in first grade about March we got a brand new school with a gym, playground equipment, and heaters that worked. My brother went for a few years to a one-room school, as did my sister. They were born in the 1940s and me in 1950.

My dad and mom were Harry Truman liberal Democrats. Most of my relatives were not. That made them a bit unpopular, but they never knew why - I did. I am more of a conservative.

My college and secondary school classes had always been popular with students. They normally liked my stories and cornball humor. I tried to be fair, fun, and forever encouraging. I always used lots of new materials and tried to get students to apply what they have learned to the real world, not always successfully. I hope and pray you will enjoy my experiences and will smile and reflect about your life. Peace be with you and read on good citizen.

The Rocks that Lifted Us Up

The days were becoming cold and dreary. Winter was on the cusp. We burned wood in those days; partly to save money, some for exercise, by mostly as an object lesson for our children. I wanted to show them that not all things are easy, but many more than less can be good.

Oh yes, my wife often helped also. Gail gathered, loaded, and usually split tons of wood with a power splitter. I cut, and hauled the big cordwood, and stacked and toted the dry wood. Well, we each did all jobs at times. On the way home, that day, we ran into some unexpected problems.

We were stuck in the mud, no doubt about it. Our van had sunk down to the axles in the mud. A trailer of wood, filled to the maximum, with freshly cut firewood. We were in the back forty nearly a half mile off the road leading home at my parents' farm near Cooper, Michigan.

My three children were with me, all under eight years old. Even at their young ages, they realized the pickle we were in. That's a fact. We tried shoveling, rocking, shoving, even crying, and nothing helped. We were mired in the mud worse than ever with darkness rapidly approaching and hope suddenly fleeting. I did what the good book asked us to all do in such situations, we all prayed together. Then like the light of a new dawn, the answer came.

The place we were stuck was in the corner of a large hay field. This field was a very familiar sight to me. Many years before I had toiled long and hard. Here as a farm youth I had picked rocks in this very hay field. The stones were plucked here by the thousands. I was paid in bologna sandwiches and groovy Kool-Aid for my efforts. Now back to the adventure.

The stones I suddenly recalled were very near our mired van. I fetched my wimping Amy and the other two rug rats, Alex and Eric. We began digging rocks out one at a time. They were hauling out the very rocks I had discarded some 33 years earlier. They were undisturbed and heaped in a pile nearly four feet tall just as I had left them in the corner of the field just at the edge of the big woods we were in. I had instructed the kids to get some rocks from the pile. The kids carried little rocks with tears dripping. They didn't understand how "dumb stones" could lift us out. Honestly, I was not sure myself that it would work, but I figured it could not hurt to try.

The children saw me as the bossy old dad at this moment. The task itself now slowly seemed to calm their tears. We now had gathered several rocks matching in size to my little son, my medium sized daughter, and largest son. I started placing the rocks in the muddy mire near the front drive wheels. They sank into the gooey mush. Still, the kids came out of the nearly dark and scary woods. One rock at a time over and over again but progress was being made. I kept putting them in the mud. The stones began to build up now the worried children looked calmer and their speed at fetching the rocks increased as they realized the dumb rocks might actually work. They now saw the plan – build up the rocks in the mud, drive on them instead of the mud and we might escape. I got into the van and drove ahead a little the van climbed again, this time, a little higher. With each forward and back motion, we rose. We repeated the process several more times, and the rocks had lifted us up. We still had a trailer full of wood mired in the mud. We unhooked it from the van. The kids clouded up again; they saw the new problem. We had driven over 60 miles worked hard cutting, stacking, and hauling wood and would bring home no firewood. They knew that was not a good thing. We made a stone path out in front of the van.

We made it through with God's help and a bit of pushing the van we might get the rest of the way out. Eric, my oldest, would have to drive the van and me the Dad would push, and maybe just maybe we could get unstuck.

Eric got a quick lesson, and I got covered with mud as he drove a bit fast, after all, we were really stuck. We had the van out of the muddy mire. The trailer, however, was still stuck full of wood. I was well pleased. I smiled to myself because I had a secret weapon new that day. It was a snatch rope. This is a large nylon rope with hooks on each end. You basically hooked on and drove off. The rope stretches like a huge rubber band and then recoils.

I backed near the trailer, told the kids to get way back. They did without hesitation. They wondered what was Dad up to now. I hooked on the trailer about 15 feet away and drove the van ahead rather rapidly. The trailer lurched ahead a couple of feet. I backed up and plunged ahead again and again until trailer and van were both free.

We celebrated when we reached the road by drinking a pop or soda. I always have a cooler loaded with them on any road trip of 20 miles or more and sometimes less. I am not always at my best in these ugly situations, but I always admit my errors and explain as best I can what went wrong and how to avoid the same mistakes in the future. We also stopped in Burger King in Kalamazoo for our usual order; Whopper Jr's all around with extra pickles plus mustard, not fries and drinks, just our cans of pop.

We rolled on home in the dark. I used my little trick at this point, put the heat on high. This puts the kids to sleep. When we turned in the driveway nearly an hour and a half later, the kids were all sound asleep.

Gail, their mother, spotted us and came out to carry in Alex, the youngest child. They all soon came alive again when we got inside, each telling their version of the rock story. The mud got deeper, the rocks they carried were all huge, and the whole situation was dire – which was true.

I hope the kids can laugh or at least smile over the entire experience some day in the future. Rocks can lift you up.

The Girl that Got the Pig's Ear

You have heard the old expression – "you finally got his ear." Well, it speaks to having someone attention. My daughter, Amy, then 13 years old at the time was soon to get the attention of one huge and stubborn hog. The kids and I were attempting to load their 4-H pigs for a short trip to the Marion Fair in Michigan. The three pigs did not want to cooperate at all. They literally had run over my eleven-year-old son, Alex, yes a 270-pound running beast crushing into you only about two feet off the ground, with a three-inch snout is a lot of power in a small place. Eric, my other son, presently fourteen years old had repeatedly attempted to control the charging hogs, but each time he was tossed aside like well-struck bowling pin. I, the father, a pretty strong 200-pound man, plus experienced farm hand, was cast off the wall onto my backside several times. Sorry to say my temper had got the best of me and I regretfully had yelled at the pigs and my kids as well. Not one of my proudest moments to be sure although we were all very upset and extremely stressed out. We were clueless as to how to get the pigs loaded up to this point, and the pigs seemed to be laughing at us. You are required to have the pigs at the fair early, and we were running out of time. In the prior three years, we had experienced no major difficulty in the process of loading up the hogs but this year the worm had turned.

That is when it happened – A. C. Penny as I sometimes call my daughter, boldly announces, "Stand back – I'll get the pig!" No one laughed or uttered a word. We stood back, and silently watched like we were caught in an old-fashioned game of frozen tag. She marched solidly and steadily down the entire length of our large pole barn. We stared in near disbelief. She carried no hog hurdle, no cane, and no show stick. These are all tools often used to aid in the control of pigs. She carried only an iron will and a strong determination. Amy was shocking us more and more with each passing second. Three strong and huge hogs still to load with each of the boys and I were totally frustrated, dirty, hurt, and feeling hopeless.

The barn radio was playing a popular country song at the time, "A girls got to do what a girl's got to do." Amy beaded in on the pig called "Ballerina" the biggest and most troubling hog this day. We were completely puzzled and still silent. She faced the pig and grasped the pig's ears one in each bare hand. The war of wills was on. Ballerina braced and squealed. Amy tugged for all she was worth. The pig inched forward, but that was a start in the right direction. Then came a sudden halt to the inching progress. Amy squatted lower and pulled with more determination. The pig whined like a sick child, but now it slowly pranced forward toward the loading ramp. We raced to join the victory march. The pig was still mad and fought back by wildly shaking its head. But even that couldn't shake A.C. My two sons, Eric and Alex, ran to push on the rear end of the pig to assist the new ranking chess queen in the battle of swineville. Then without warning the pig crap got us all stationed in the rear guard. It shot out like smelly, burnt rocket fuel. The three of us were on the wrong end at the wrong time. Commander Amy showed no sign of retreat in the hog wars. We were now winning, and Ballerina was giving up. The pace quickened, and we were now halfway to our stock trailer. Still, no one smiled even as our goal was getting closer by the second. Amy reached the ramp and continued straight up the ramp into the trailer. Eric quickly slammed the tailgate shut, and the first of the pigs was now loaded. Amy glanced at us and headed back to the barn floor battlefield. She immediately targeted her second pig. I, of course, can't read a pig's mind, but they are known to be rather smart. The second pig had lost much of its will to resist.

Apparently, a once squealing now loaded hog on the trailer had had an effect on the second, once crabby litter mate. Amy then grabbed it by the ears as well and single-handedly walked the second of the three pigs across the barn and again directly right into the trailer without hesitation.

The third pig must have lost all its nerve to fight too. Believe it or not, it loaded itself. It walked – no trotted – across the barn floor then up the ramp into the stock trailer with the two other pigs. Apparently, it wanted no part of a girl with a strong will and lots of desire to finish a troubling job that needed to be done.

We each smiled proudly and congratulated Amy for a job well done. She showed a level of courage and confidence that each of us would never forget. The kids did well at the fair pig show that year, thankfully. They each successfully sold their pigs at the 4-H auction sale for a good price and used the money to pay a small portion of their expenses years later as they each attended Michigan State University, graduating with GPAs around 3.5 and up.

Raising swine has its rewards and lessons that can last a lifetime. That being you don't know what you can do with a lot of determination and a strong desire to do your best.

That was the last year of raising pigs at our small farm, and now only our garden misses them. The memories you share are more fun as the old stories get retold and we learn to laugh at ourselves.

Ice Fishing My Way

Ice fishing can have many purposes. Sure there is the sport and challenge. I did not know much about walking on water, but I know now with a little ice under our feet we all can do it.

Several years ago, my life's journey turned crazy. God took me to the edge of death twice, first in 2000 and again in 2001.

Blood clots traveled through my heart and settled in my lungs twice. The odds of living through two Bilateral Pulmonary Embolism episodes is only about 3%. You have to have a lot of talks with yourself when you're in a deep valley. If you are blessed, you review everything, ask the question "why me?" and then you realized it can't be answered.

In the end, you decide that having a nice Christian family is about as good as it gets, you asked God what his plans for you are, and you go fishing for your answer.

Oh yes, about the ice fishing not much equipment is needed. Two or three poles are best. I fish a lot while standing up. Dean and Butch, a couple of nice fellows I met on the ice, taught me the basics. You catch a lot more fish that way. You change depths more, and you will naturally jig more while standing.

Sitting down too much can make you get lazy. You need a short, very flexible pole, three and a half to five feet long to use this method.

Most of us "standards" hot glue a flat of very light wire springs unto the end of the pole. It should be placed so that the spring is glued on slightly past the end of the tip a half an inch is good.

I use high visibility 2# gold line. Then you wear bifocals like me it's easier to see when you break off your tear drop and have to tie on a new one. I use green with gold flecks most often size 12 or 14. You can use size 10 as well. Other colors I use at times are pink, purple, and orange.

I use a small open-faced reel, but if you're fishing in water of 18 feet or less it's not necessary. It can actually slow you down if it's colder than about 20 degrees. At that temperature or below it freezes up quickly on your reel.

The purest simply lift the pole above their heads and back away from the hole they don't use reels at all. This gets the fish out of the hole quickly. That is critical because when the fish pass your way, it often does not last very long and the fish are gone again. The idea is to catch them and drop back down as soon as possible.

You only use one pole while standing. When I sit down, I use two short poles with the same hot glued on wire spring and a very small open faced reel. I use very light action 30-inch poles most times. You will lose more fish this way, but you'll get more bites.

I suggest using two different color tear drops to see if it makes a difference. I have used ant tear drops but again it's not necessary. I do frequently tie on two tear drops on each pole when I sit down to fish. I put them 8 to 12 inches apart. It is not a good idea for first times because you can catch the upper tear drop under the ice quite often and you'll lose the fish and both tear drops. You might get mad or sad when that happens because it can be your favorites lures.

I use only spikes for bait. They are tough. I buy 1000 at a time and keep them in the garage or fridge if I don't get caught. That's enough bait to harvest at least 500 panfish if you go fishing enough.

You can use minnows or wax worms, as well to catch panfish. They all work, but three years and 60 trips out on the ice taught me simple is good. I use a small container to hold my spikes; it's called a bait puck by strike master. Chewing tobacco cans and empty pill bottles are also good for live bait. It is best to keep them warmed up in your pocket they'll be more lively on your hook.

I place up to four dangling spikes on my hook. The plastic containers they come in at the bait store is a very bad idea. It will crush in your pocket, and your bait will be killed. You'll be forced to waste a lot of time getting more bait, and it takes the fun away.

Other good ideas are to carry your poles in a plastic pail with a plastic ice scoop, a small hard container for extra lures, and a few bottles of water or pop. Warm pop is a good idea. If you want to drink it soon, lay it on the ice. Otherwise, leave it in your pail so it won't freeze up so fast.

I use two pails; one can be used as a seat. You'll need an ice auger, a 5-inch laser is an excellent choice, and it's black in color. Small ones are good for pan fishing its faster cutting but tip up fishing requires an 8-inch diameter hole. A good way to keep people from getting around you so fast is to hide the fish you catch. A 5-quart empty ice cream pail with a slit in the top works well.

Get on out there and enjoy God's great outdoors and you might catch your supper.

The Horse That Got Away

Horses are not always nice – any real horse lover would agree with that statement.

Horses do not plan to be mean and nasty; it's just part of their instinct or nature. True cowboys and cowgirls are optimists. They always believe that their horses will obey and do what they, the rider, leader, or driver, wants them to do. The facts are often contrary. Humans can and do become injured while attempting to ride normally friendly, but sometimes crazy, four-legged friends.

My farm country story today is another true story. I will share a couple of rides down the lane that no one present can forget- even if they tried.

The day was fair, warm, and sunny not a cloud to be seen. Sunday afternoon you felt glad to be alive, and you had the time to enjoy the Lord's Day. The huge sweet cherry trees were in full bloom. Their leaves were gently waving in the breeze. Sweet smells were in the air. We eagerly anticipated the rides we would have on our new horse that day.

All three Johnson children and the neighbor boy, Paul, were assembled and eager for their turn. We all helped saddle-up our horse, Sookey, a former thoroughbred race horse. My parents had not rescued a horse like this before. It was an animal bred to run and run fast. We saw a calm and gentle horse standing before us.

We each watched my sister, Pat, mount up on our horse without much trouble. Then the horse suddenly started prancing as if it were ready for a big race. Pat looked more like she was strapped on board a rocket headed for Mars. The crazy beast ran right under the nearest cherry tree. My sister ducked at the last second. She hit into the limbs but stayed on, which was good for green rider off to a wicked start through no fault of her own.

The horse was flying as Pat leaned forward and grabbed for the mane. The wild sucker turned north and headed down the lane at full speed. Then we saw her disappear over a hill. The three of us stood frozen glancing at each other with sheer horror in our eyes and hearts. Was that going to be the last time we would ever see my sister alive again? We could not believe our eyes. We knew all too well that it's not possible to dismount a galloping horse. We were inexperienced, but we did realize that fact. What to do was our dilemma: go after her or wait.

Horse are smart enough to return home when a rider is lost. Fresh water, hay, and oats are three good reasons to come back. We knew that much – after all, we had seen TV shows like Gene Autry and the Lone Ranger. We could sometimes hear the hooves beating along. We had assembled down the lane a short distance trying to decide what to do. Gary, my older brother, said we should close the gate to trap the horse in the barnyard if it came by. We now could hear the beating hooves getting louder by the second. We took that as possible good news.

The now lopping steed crested the last hill and headed toward us. We could see my sister Pat laying down on Sookey but not moving. We grasped in unison. Each of us knew now we had to get out of the lane so that the horse could pass and not turn back. All three boys dove under the fences on each side of the cattle lane. The lathered horse calmly trotted past. We got quickly up, raced behind and closed the gate. Doing so would enclose the horse into a smaller area.

Then the runaway horse simply stopped in its tracks. Brother Gary and I carefully and cautiously approached. Pat slowly slid down the tall horse. Our eager arms caught the exhausted heroine. She was sweaty, pale, breathless and wild-eyed. How she was ever able to stay on the horse was remarkable. The horse stood like an old plow horse at the end of a day's work in the field. Pat either could not or chose not to talk at all. Gary and I waited quietly to hear her story.

Paul, the neighbor boy, led the horse away from us. His next action was so unexpected you could never have guessed or anticipated it. He was starting to mount the horse. He was nearly up when it happened. The horse bolted again, the saddle loosened and Paul was in the saddle, yet was on the side of the galloping beast.

He could not hold on, and he hit the ground with a thud. This was looking like some weird circus trick, but we knew it was a desperate and dangerous situation. Off ran the horse and this time, the rider was not on top but being dragged underneath with one foot caught in the stirrup. The lane gate was closed this time, but would Sookey stop?

Paul was in a panic. The ground changed from a smooth grassy area to gut wrenching ruts. He screamed for help, but we could not catch up to the running frightened horse.

We all gave chase and ran for all we were worth. The closed gate was coming up quickly. We were scared to death wondering what the once glue factory bound, crazed beast would do next, no one knew. Then as suddenly as a gust of wind, the horse stopped at the gate. Sookey then turned her head back whinnied and gently nudged Paul. The once bouncing boy was still struggling to free his foot from the stirrup.

His face, arms, and legs looked horrible. He had suffered a major case of road rash. Why he had not been crushed by the pounding hooves is a question only God can answer. I asked Paul if he was badly hurt. He moaned and said, "I'll be ok – I just need a few minutes."

Paul offered the answer to the question we all shared in silence. He said he thought Sookey would be too tired to run fast again. Well, that proved to be a bad assumption. He paid a heavy price for his decision that day. I wonder if he ever got up on another horse.

No one ever showed any interest in riding that horse again. We put the horse away in the barn. We gave it a brief wipe off and brushed it all over. We then headed for the house. My mom saw us coming. As it usually happened, we all stood mute for a time but at long last, I spoke up. Breaking the silence first, I learned the hard way, is not such a good idea. I ended up taking the harshest punishment from mom, but the horse did, I suppose, even things up for all but Gary. He had a knack for avoiding the brunt of these situations. That's a skill I never mastered as a child. I foolishly admitted that I had wanted to ride the horse.

The others said nothing and that was often a theme repeated throughout my early days. Even now the others remember things differently than me. I recall the stories with ease and when we get together my brothers and sister, however, can't seem to find pleasant, fun stories in their memories to share.

The rest of the story is rather nice. The very next day my dad and mom trucked away the horse called Sookey. He was sold to a mink farm. It is best now to forget about the horse completely. They must have gotten a good price for the horse from hell because we were given the best surprise of all my childhood. We each were allowed to pick out new bikes in Kalamazoo, at a real bike shop, not one from the hardware store. I really enjoyed that bike. Gary and I rode the tires off those bikes several times. We would commonly ride our one-speed bikes ten miles or more at a time. Some Sundays we would ride up to thirty miles in a day. We were healthy kids that worked hard on our farm six days a week. The horse got away twice, and it got taken away once and for all.

Some Sheep Stories

Dogs and sheep often do not mix.

Sure a good sheep dog is more valuable than gold to a sheep man. You saw that first hand when you lived on a large sheep farm in the 50s and 60s. However, once a stray dog bites a sheep and tastes blood – it's not good. We had to deal with that situation a lot, and it's best not to dwell on that anymore.

We had 250 ewes and produced 450 lambs per year or more. Sheep rearing takes lots of TLC, and you need to help a lot during lambing season. Sheep do not wear watches, so helping with birthing at 3 a.m. is rather common.

The weather is a powerful and unpredictable enemy, chilling newborn lambs. Stressed lambs can get in trouble quickly. Cold spring weather kills them if it's too cold and/or too windy. Sheep need help and shepherds have been the people doing the work with the not so bright animals for hundreds of years.

Rams, male sheep, are strong and can be mean and dangerous. My sister once raised an orphan ram lamb. Its mother died and my sister, Pat, begged my parents to allow her to raise up the lamb. She got her wish, and we all experienced the lessons.

Pat had to put milk in a bottle and warmed it up several times per day. The lamb got to live in the house for a week or so. A pet, of course, needs a name, so my sister chose, "Frisky!"

The lamb grew very fast and became a pest. It followed everyone around and actually would sneak outside rather often. We all played games with the lamb. We would hide around the house, and Frisky would try to find us. Hide and seek with a sheep seems funny and it was.

Lambs like to bounce around stiff legged like they are on four pogo sticks when they feel good, and a warm spring breeze is in the air. It can make a crabby person laugh and when you live on a farm that is surely appreciated.

My sister even dressed-up the lamb and put him in a baby buggy like he was riding in a parade. The lamb was eventually put out in the pens with the other sheep after a few weeks. He still bugged you when you went out to feed or water other sheep. It was because he had no fear of humans because of his upbringing. Frisky bumped your water pails and made you spill your water. That caused you extra work because it made you make extra trips.

If you have hundreds of sheep, pigs, and cattle to care for, the humor or extra work loses its luster rather quickly. It took my brother and I close to two hours to do chores each morning and night. Gary, my brother, got tired of having Frisky mess with him. So he started hitting him each time the growing lamb bumped him during feeding. That went fine for a couple of months. The young ram grew large by late fall, then it got even.

Gary was carrying two large pails of water into the sheep barn. I was bringing the grain in a couple of pails right behind him. I admit I was afraid of Frisky by then. Gary went up the four steps with the water. He got blasted and flew back out like a rocket. He flew completely past the steps onto the ground. Then the ram came in for seconds. Lucky for Gary, he still had empty buckets in hand and fended off the ram with a couple of good raps. Gary was not hurt much except possibly his pride. It was somewhat funny to watch because Gary had just bragged how he had trained the young ram to stay back. You can never relax around farm animals that are large and old enough to mate. Frisky the ram certainly lived up to his name.

The second part of this story involves a dangerous Suffolk ram. My dad and I were down to our basement barn that we rented next door. Dad spotted a couple of newborn lambs that were not in the maternity pens. My dad swept them up into his big Swedish arms. The frightened looking lambs were looking for their mother and started bleating. That is a cry for help, and the big guy answered that call. Our huge ram crashed into my dad and blew him through a ¾ inch thick wooden wall. My dad screamed in pain and fear. The blow had knocked him silly. I was up in the hay mound dropping bales down. I never had heard my dad scream in my entire life. I knew instantly terrible troubles were brewing. I jumped and dropped through the floor down with the bales. The ram cracked him again and again when he was down.

My fears subsided, and God gave me a plan. I used a hay bale to shield me from the crazed ram. Luckily for me, my rush toward the ram confused him for a moment. He backed off not knowing what I was up to. Honestly, I had no idea of what I was doing. My dad cleared his head and dragged himself to safety. I guarded my dad from the ram, but he had backed off. The twin lambs were lost in the attack. My dad was very badly bruised and stunned. Why this stuff happens no one can say.

My dad seemed to lose some interest in sheep farming after that day. I certainly could understand his feeling after that experience. You don't commonly think of sheep as dangerous until you live through situations where someone could have been killed. Farming was and still is a very dangerous job if you are not very careful.

Raising Geese and Turkeys

It was 1957. I was seven years old. You did whatever we farmers could think of to make a little money.

Those days may have returned in 2007, fifty years later. Sometimes it was quite a struggle and the work required was difficult. The difference then was you took a longer view, and you expected no free lunch. Today many people think they are entitled to the nice things they really do not need – like cell phones, satellite TV, computers, etc. A good book from the library would be better for many.

Raising geese is quite an experience. They do not follow the rules of being nice and play fair. They like to do their own thing and go where they please when they please. My family raised these birds for a Greek restaurant in Kalamazoo, the city where I was born.

We had both white and gray geese. That may seem odd except they were Pilgrim geese – the males are white, and the females are gray and white or two-toned. The males get up to 14 pounds and females about 13 pounds.

Both males and females were sassy and hissed when you wanted them to do things they wanted no part of. We got the nice cute goslings, but that phase only lasted a couple of weeks. You had to go out into the pen to fill the large, round, gravity type grain feeders daily and water pans as well.

Geese are not as smart as pigs – they crap all over the place. Pigs poop in one area and unlike dogs, they don't lay in poop unless they are forced to do so for lack of space. You simply can't avoid the wet slippery mess that geese leave behind. The smell is strong, especially when it rains.

Wild animals do not bother geese like they do turkeys. I believe the loud noises they make scares away many predatory animals. Plus, you do not have to teach geese teamwork. If they are threatened, they all go after the bad guys together.

Geese are buggers because they crowd you a lot if the feeders get dry. You always wanted to avoid spilling since Dad liked to inspect your work from time to time. So you are trying to be so darn careful that you lost track of where the geese were. The results often were part of your butt got taken away in an instant. It hurts like a place found near Ann Arbor. The worse part being that you had to go back in there the next day and face those orange bills again. I believe it may be part of the reason my back side is small today compared to my overall size. It's because part of me is missing after being around all those mean geese as a kid.

Eventually, my mom got tired of butchering our geese. It was decided that the best thing to do was sell them live. That still left a dreaded job; catching the geese and putting them into the transport cages. You had to crowd them into one corner of the pen and grab them up. Their long necks caused you big problems. All you could do to protect yourself was to wear several layers of clothing and thick leather gloves.

I hated those monsters, a goose had just bitten me in the ear. I start to cry, but my dad told me to be tough and stop weeping. The verbal criticism stopped a few days later when I was gone for the weekend. My dad volunteered to feed the full grown geese for my birthday. I got to be at my loving grandmother Lida's house.

My older brother, Gary, secretly told me that he had heard Swedish words he had never heard before when I was gone. The geese project ended shortly after that day. Wimpy Dale, it turned out, wasn't making up those tall tales about the big mean geese after all. Gary and I sure didn't miss them biting us and hissing at us all the time.

The bad part came next. We had all the feeders, crowd pens, and other gear sitting around not doing any good with little use for them. That's when the huge white Holland turkeys came home to replace the geese. The red foxes really enjoyed those young poults.

My great Uncle Glenn taught us some old school ways to scare the foxes away. He told us to put smelly work clothes up on the posts in the turkey yard. It did great for a while then the foxes got wise and ignored the clothing and ate up a lot of our young turkeys.

My brother, Gary, got to check the trap lines with my uncle as a result of the fox issue. Foxes had a $5 State of Michigan bounty on them at the time, plus people actually wore fox pelts. My great uncle easily sold all the pelts he trapped.

Next came another enemy to our turkeys, weasels. They dug in and lived under the barn. They didn't try anything with the geese. We had slowed down the foxes and still the flock of turkeys continued to decline. We trapped them out and poisoned their dens. Weasels are crazy tough varmints.

I did like raising turkeys a little more than geese but not much. My older brother, Gary, and I again were the caretakers of the turkeys. Some of the same negatives came up; crap everywhere and when the turkeys got big they scared me. The big hungry turkeys often gobbled loudly, and the growing toms or males start strutting about. You were not so sure what they could do to you, and I had no interest in finding out.

Turkeys were hard to handle just like the geese had been when it was time to butcher them out. My dad and his family had worked with chickens a lot but not with geese or turkeys. We struggled handling and raising both. The turkeys pecked us and tried to spur us. It was not enjoyable.

I have some good memories on the farm; mean geese and turkeys are not one of them. I now realize my parents were struggling to be successful and to make money farming. They did not try to stress us, boys, out, but it sure was difficult at times. We quit trying to raise geese and turkeys after this on a grand basis.

Thanks be to God that I never got hurt severely on the farm, but I sure had a lot of close calls. If you haven't experienced some of these situations, it's hard to make you feel what it felt like. I pray your trip down farm lane helps you get a sense of the days and times of the past.

The Boar Got Hammered

Swine are interesting farm animals, yet they can be difficult to handle and raise. We had about 30 breed- gilts and sows in our breeding herd at our farm most of the time. My dad liked the Yorkshire and Landrace breeds of swine best. We had Hampshire and Duroc swine at times also. Our family converted our old stanchion dairy barn to birthing swine pens. We started with tearing out all the old equipment and rewiring it for the needed heat lamps. My dad had milked cows until the milk inspector insisted we had to put in lots of new concrete and a bulk milk tank. We had the highest quality milk in a seven county area of southwestern Michigan. My dad was known as a stubborn Swede at times. He did not want to spend the money when he was doing a good job as it was. Milk cans were heavy and hard to handle. They weighed about 98 pounds when full, they held 10 gallons of milk. Technology was coming and if you pump out the milk no one had to pick up those back breaking, heavy cans again.

Embracing change can be difficult and scary. My dad also really did not like the seven days a week, twice a day, no breaks work. You could find people to feed and water pigs for a few days, but few who would or could milk all your cows properly. Farmers today make the same claim nearly 50 years later. My dad seemed to like raising pigs, and he had a lively and caring mentor, my great uncle, Gordon. He was a giant of a man, a stout German and he was normally very gentle. He was seventy years old, but his arms looked like those of a professional wrestler of the 21st century.

We started the pig raising, but the winter cold created a couple of difficult seasons. The water froze up when it got below 10 degrees Fahrenheit. It was difficult to water the animals and clean out the pens as a result. We closed the barn in better, and we put heat tape on our pipes. We also squeezed in a few more pigs and that actually increased the temperature in the barn which helped the entire situation.

My dad, and us kids got all the operation running smoother each week, and the pigs saved per litter got high enough that MSU's swine specialist came to view our operation. We all learned and applied all the lessons we could. My dad used to give the sows a small amount of coal. It seemed to help - it was an old secret brought over from Germany from Great Uncle Gordon. Today it would be likely considered as part of using micro-nutrients in swine feeding. My dad was getting pretty proud and bold at this point, and he wanted to top the market with his pigs. That is to say, he always wanted to get the highest price of all the pigs at the market on any given day. He normally was close, but not always there. My mom needed to be consulted if Dad wanted to go spend a lot of money. My dad had heard about a $250 Yorkshire boar; he believed it could elevate his herd to the level he dreamed about. We got the boar in early spring. My uncle Gordon told my dad to keep the boar inside for a couple of days, and he would come over and help my dad put a ring in its nose. Sorry to say, my dad did not listen to my mom's uncle. That's when the troubles began.

    The beautiful boar came from a fancy farm where all the pigs were kept on cement. The large, strong boar was out on the ground for the first time in its life. Instinct took over, and the animal rooted like a plow tractor. That was why Gordon strongly advised the nose ring to stop the rooting. I saw a major problem happening when I was slopping the hogs. The new boar was rapidly rooting out the brace post that held up the end of a forty-foot section of our barn.

I knew better than to go in with a 400 pound plus boar to try to scare him away. Plus a few years earlier Gordon's daughter Sally had been nearly killed when she fell off her horse and got knocked-out in a swine-yard. The fall got her bleeding, and the pigs tried to eat her alive. I saw the hundreds of stitches she had all over her body. It wasn't pretty. She spent several months in the hospital. No way would I challenge a huge mean beast.

I ran up to get my dad before the barn collapsed. My dad had been doing carpenter work at the house next door. He sternly walked out to the swine barn. The boar was indeed about to take out the support post. The sight of the rooting boar got my dad boiling mad. He drew out his 20-ounce claw hammer and whipped it at the rooting boar hog. It was a direct hit in the head. The pig dropped in a heap. My dad was totally shocked and now panicked. We both cautiously approached the now motionless boar. Dad lifted its head; it just flopped back down. No sign of life at all. My dad headed back to the house, his head was down, and his shoulders slumped. I said nothing. I got the loader tractor out and was about to remove the boar from the barn. I glanced into where the boar laid. No pig there, but then I spotted the stumbling boar walking away like a drunken sailor. I dashed into the house and found my dad crying along with my mother. This was a very rare moment. I blurted out, "the boar is alive! It was only knocked out. It's okay now, I think." We all briskly walked out and viewed the still stunned hog. It was a happy moment. God has a funny way of teaching people lessons. That day's was - don't throw a hammer at our prized pig because losing your temper can have a steep price to pay.

My dad had a visit from Uncle Gordon later that day. It was a mixture of good-hearted ribbing and I-told-you-so. The cement forms went up that week and the concrete filled the back end of the barn. No more support post problems and the boar got some nice brass looking jewelry, a nose ring. The story with its odd humor now lives on here in print. I hope it gave you a little diversion and couple of grins.

Indian Trees and Great Grandma's Stories

The Zen of seeing is a skill you can hone. The basic gist or use here is that two people looking at the same situation or thing will view things differently. The simplest way to think of things around Northern Michigan is many local people traveling about will see whitetail deer rather easily in an instant. People visiting from non-rural areas might be riding in the same car and never see any deer. My great grandmother Josephine Smith Layton told me a few stories about her life around American Indians. She lived in Southwestern Michigan. She was born around 1865. A small tribe of Blackfoot Indians lingered around her small country home. She told me stories about her mother making fresh bread, then setting it on the window ledge to cool. She later went to bring in the cooled bread and found no bread. The next day the empty baking tins were returned. Raccoons are smart wild animals, but even they probably couldn't do that. It was believed, at first, to be a prank by her husband, John Smith.

Not wanting to go along with the prank Grandma Jo's mother said nothing to her husband. This story repeated itself for four days, and her patience wore thin. She caved but to her surprise and dismay her husband knew nothing. He thought maybe she was mad at him and refused to make him the bread he loved so much. Things were getting a bit crazy now. He was selling all the milk from their three cows in a small nearby village, Alamo. So now no butter could be churned by his wife.

The showdown finally came. Grandma said, "Why are you messing with my bread and now you're selling all the milk leaving none to make butter that we use on the bread." Grandpa was left clueless. He stated he had no idea about the cause for the missing bread. The bread was put out again the following day, and the mystery was solved.

Then came a new situation to deal with- light-fingered Indians. Later that afternoon a new piece to the puzzle was revealed. A freshly cleaned wild rabbit was left in the empty bread tin and placed back on the window sill where the bread was left to cool that morning.

It was determined to play out the situation a bit further. My great great grandmother and father decided to continue to put the bread out but at a reduced rate of one loaf every other day or so. People in those days normally baked one or two times per week. If you sold bread or had a large family you, of course, baked more frequently. Then the bread situation took another odd step. First was the fresh rabbit now came a fox squirrel all cleaned and fresh, again left in the empty bread pan.

My relatives told a few friends about the growing developments. Several gave them stern warnings and told them scary tales about people who had befriended Indians to their demise. My ancestors were professed Christians so they prayed and drew up their own plans. By their own admission, they had no prior experience to guide them. It was spring, and the Indians had not been around during the winter. It was determined that these people may be travelers of sorts suffering hard times.

Great Great Grandpa Smith decided to take a leap of faith. When the Indians came up for the new bread, he invited them into his house. They cautiously shuffled in. His wife had made stew out of the wild game adding home grow potatoes, carrots, and turnips stored under the house in the root cellar. The hungry Indians partook of the warm meal with grateful hearts. They could not talk to each other, but a sharing bond was formed somehow.

The entire small band arrived the following day include a couple of small children. My great grandma

Josephine, then about four-year-old, asked if she could play with the Indian children. Her mother consented and likewise the Indian children were set free to join her. It didn't take long, and the kids were catching frogs near the creek just behind the cottage. The leopard frogs can be great fun. Most can leap two or three feet per hop, and the laughter broke the remaining tension.

Smiles replaced frowns and tension was replaced with common respect. One of the younger teenage Indians, it turned out, actually spoke limited English.

The Indians offered some dried meat similar to the jerky to my people, and it was cheerfully accepted. Out of curiosity, the Indians were asked why they had decided to camp in this area. They told my relatives about seeing an Indian tree just up the path. Most people now call them Trail Marker Trees. Native Americans bent over young saplings hardwoods usually: White Oak, American Elms, and Red Maple trees. They then staked or tied the stem down to the ground with vines or rawhide. The goal was to create a trained trunk. It hopefully would grow parallel to the ground.

Some Trail Marker Trees were used to indicate to indigenous people that a good camp site, an easy water crossing was nearby, or possibly even that a nice lovely spring was present to get some fresh water. The Indians showed my people a true secret and asked them not to share the information. Josephine, my great grandmother, only told me when she was nearly 90 years old. Even now I am hesitant to share this information. Back then, not having the trees to guide them could have caused huge delays or even death if it were late in the fall or during the early winter. Had non-trustworthy people known what they were and what their purpose was the trees might have been cut down.

My family continued to get along well with the Indians with no problems. Eventually, the Indians moved on heading farther west. As an Agriculture and Natural Resource Instructor at the Career Tech Center in Cadillac, I used to tell this tale of the Indian Trees around mushroom hunting season. We had several such trees on the school's nearly 200 acres near the Clam River. The students would come in all excited within a few days telling me about sighting some Indian trees, and that was such fun.

See if you can develop a Zen of seeing if you know what you're looking for. I tried out my basic story around

Marion and showed people what they look like from an internet picture. Most everyone claimed to have seen at least one of them at some point in time. No one seemed to know that it might mean something special or maybe even something spiritual to American Indians.

Happy hunting this spring and I hope you enjoyed your trip now armed with new information. Mushrooms are still more fun to find than seeing trees with new eyes.

Tractors Can Fly

The weather dictated our actions that day.

The old timers always said, "Make hay while the sun shines." It was early June and a lite breeze rippled through the nearby leaves and the nicely glowing sun was drying the hay rapidly. It looked like it would be ready to be baled in the early afternoon.

All was well it seemed when the wheels started falling off the wagon, so to say. The timing chain broke on our hay baler. My dad was working at Quality Farm and Fleet.

That left me in charge with a repair situation beyond my experience.

The problems started to mount up. I called the equipment dealership, but the field serviceman had just had surgery. He would come out with the needed parts, and with his direction, I had to do the actual repairs. We still had three full loads of hay stacked on the wagons from the day before, ready to be unloaded. We were short our usual tractor driver as he was sick that day, or at least he was sick of hauling hay. That shortfall of an experienced helper created a difficult situation for me, the acting farm manager. I was 15 years old.

If the baler had not broken down, it would have been me taking the load down to the hay barn. I called in my best friend's brother, Jerry White, to help out that day. He normally worked with a neighborhood farmer also hauling hay but was not needed that day. So I was able to use him which was a good break since he knew how to work.

It was often difficult to find people willing to earn their pay even in 1965. They wanted the money, but many didn't realize how hot, heavy, and tough stacking and throwing 60 - 80 lbs. bales can be. You put in eight hours or more baking in the sun or an airless hayloft with lots of dust blowing or crawling into your eyes. The same ugly dust always sticking to your sweaty skin like glue. It just was not that much fun. Yes, it could make you stronger and more resilient.

Eating humble pie can have its long term benefits, and if you fall off a bouncing wagon with a bale in your arms several times, you learn to concentrate better. Stepping into various holes or tripping on the strings while carrying bales to the back corner of the barn tested your determination and maybe even your character.

Bales also have a very nasty habit - they get heavier as the day wears on. Your once sure grip on the strings, or much worse, the wires, gets to both your mind and your body.

Oh yes, back to the main story. Jerry, my new worker that day, volunteered to drive the tractor and full load of hay down to the barn to unload the first wagon. We usually used a small Johnny Popper, a JD 420, to pull the wagons down to the barn from the fields. But that day we were using a larger Case 801 diesel. It made me a bit nervous, but he seemed confident and said he had driven loads of hay into a barn at the other farmer's place.

I was stuck since the high-priced, service mechanic had just arrived. The two hired hands and my 10-year brother, Chris, could start emptying the wagons while I fixed the baler.

Jerry backed up to the load while Chris dropped the pin through the hitch, clipped the hair pin through the draw pin and away they went.

I went to work with the serviceman to replace the timing chain and retime the baler so the plunger wouldn't sheer off the knotting needles.

All was going swimmingly when it hit the fan. My brother arrived into the hay field where we were fixing the baler with a very labored walk, holding his back. His eyes were glazed and teary with a look of sheer terror.

"What was wrong?" I demanded to know. Chris replied, "Jerry drove the tractor out the back of the barn. I jumped off the top of the wagon and landed on a barn beam."

"My God what happened to Jerry?"

"I don't know," stated Chris.

"Can you make it up to the house to get mom?"

The wise mechanic, by then, had already started his truck and waved me in.

He said, "You just tell me where to go." I did, and in a couple of minutes we arrived.

The tractor was nowhere to be seen, and Jerry was missing. I called for him but got no answer. The hay wagon still full of bales teetered on the edge of a 12-foot drop. It was a drive up style barn, with an earthen ramp.

"Oh my God, where was Jerry?" I thought he most likely had been crushed to death by the tractor. I ran to check out the scene and spotted the now stalled tractor. It ran into dad's new corn planter and died there. That was good, at least it wasn't loose, headed for US 131, less than a quarter a mile away.

Still no sign of Jerry. Then I spotted the lifeless body hanging by one leg under the still full wagon of hay. Mom, God, or both were sending help. It was arriving in waves now.

People flocked in off the road - all asking what they could do. I took over like I knew what I was doing. I didn't.

Somehow, as if by instinct, I assigned jobs in an instant. First, we chained the wagon to a beam so it couldn't come the rest of the way out the barn's drop off.

People, many of whom I did not know, jumped up onto the severely tilted wagon without regard for their personal safety and tossed the remaining bales off. It was as if a troop of angels was at work.

I sent a lady I never met to a nearby house to call for the ambulance. She struck off without hesitation, and we soon heard the siren approaching in the distance. We were still not out of the woods yet. Then Jerry started to murmur.

He was in pain but seemed to calm down when I told him we would get him out soon. I had no fear there under the front of the wagon for some reason. The ambulance arrived, but they showed no inclination of going underneath the wagon to help.

I asked the guys around me to help lift the wagon up, off Jerry. No one uttered a word, they simply stepped up to an edge and the wagon, raised it up, and I carried Jerry to the waiting stretcher.

He didn't look that bad - only cut up a bit. Somehow his leg busted off a barn board, about to the width of his leg, and it was more struck than crushed.

If that wagon had continued out the side of the barn, it would have cut him in two. Why nothing more happened to Jerry that day only one knows.

The tractor did a 360, lost its oil, and died. The corn planter was trashed. My brother's back eventually recovered. He later played high school sports and college basketball.

Jerry was kept one night in the hospital and sent home. His mother died recently, and we met at the visitation.

We rehashed the story. It changed his life, he told me, and he never again took things for granted. He is a fine Christian man with a lovely wife of 25 years and nice Christian children.

They all were there to support their dad that day. What more can anyone ask for? Tractors can fly, but they generally are not meant to.

Yumping Yimminy

That's the way I heard the news from the long fishing dock across the lake. We were on Payne Lake near Yankee Springs State Recreation area close to Middleville, Michigan.

It was a beautiful summer day. My Grandmother Layton was hosting my Grandfather Johnson for an afternoon of fishing. Both were known to enjoy a nice day on the water. My grandma was famous on the lake for always being able to catch fish no matter the day or time.

My Grandfather Johnson came to the United States directly from Sweden via Ellis Island in New York. He didn't know any English, so even the process of talking to the authorities there was difficult.

My sister tried to track down the names of our relatives from the old country and learned he simply chose the name closest to his name as he could understand. My name actually should not be the common name Johnson. I am not sure what it should be. I think perhaps it is Jonson. My sister is the only one that knows at this point. That is the reason for the odd title to this story. Yumping Yimminy.

Since he was actually trying to say, "jumping jiminy" or something like it.

My grandmother had hooked a very large bass. She was using a 20-foot-long fiberglass pole. The fish was so huge that even from far away you could hear the fish line singing and whining.

Lida's pole was bending in an extreme manner. The battle was on and the excitement was building. Grandpa realized the fishing net would be needed, but it was at the front end of the boat and to get it he would have to get past grandma.

It was a small, narrow row boat. He was about 85 years old that day in 1960. A fish that large, of course, could not be fully controlled. It went under the boat, around the boat, towards shore and Lida kept the tip up and the pressure on the fish.

Grandpa Johnson squeezed past and got the net. The boat was rocking, and the fish was starting to get tired. Grandma Lida told Grandpa Johnson to hoist scoop him out when he comes up close. The fish got close, but the fish saw the net and dug to the bottom of the lake.

The line was singing again, but it was getting quieter again. The fish was now jumping completely out of the water. The fish shook and thrashed, but it was still hooked somehow, but its will was lost. John, my grandpa, netted the fish, and in his Swedish brogue he gasped, "By yin it's a big fish!" What a show I saw.

Stories and a great life shared with a loving and caring family are so important. God has sent me many trials, but his grace trumps it all.

Sox Saves Some Sheep

Did you ever have a loyal dog? Our farm had such a dog – it was a Standard Collie, a Lassie look-alike, named Sox.

We raised sheep, mostly Suffolks, black-faced sheep. Several other area farms were active in purebred sheep farming as breeders of top notch sheep.

It takes years to gain a foothold in this very competitive business. The only way to speed up the process in 1962 was to buy your way in. My dad and mom took a chance. They rolled the dice and tried to help my sister, Pat, get a couple super sheep.

The fine sheep came from an exclusive sale at Michigan State University. They cost $500 for just two young ewes. Even back then it would equal about $3,000 in today's money. Today cloning and artificial insemination can do the job in months.

Our farm was only seven miles north of Kalamazoo, a city of 60,000 people. Many new homeowners had freshly moved into the countryside. They thought they could simply allow their dogs to freely roam the hills and dales.

They either did not know or did not care about the potential dangers of such a careless act.

Michigan law states no dog is allowed to be left loose. We have what is referred to as the leash law – dogs are to be tied or penned up at all times.

It was Easter Sunday, and we had just come home from church. We heard the sound of fiercely barking and growling dogs out near the cattle barn silo. My brother, Gary and I ran out to see what the uproar was all about. When we arrived, Sox, our dog had a very large German Shepherd pinned to the ground.

Unfortunately, there were two other dogs chasing and chewing the sheep. Dozens of sheep lay dead or dying in the barnyard. We both immediately jumped into the pen and started yelling and chasing the mean and murderous dogs.

My dad hurriedly showed up with a shotgun, but the dogs were far away by then. He shot off a couple of rounds, but the dogs were out of range.

We called the sheriff, but they didn't show up for an hour or so. They said that it was a shame, but believed it was hopeless unless we could tell them who owned the dogs and where they could be located. We were treated as if we were second-class citizens.

We never got a penny from all the losses. My sister Pat was hurt the most. Her flock that took her nearly ten years to build up was lost in an hour. She had 35 beautiful purebred sheep when we left for church, and only 8 were left alive when we got home, and 4 of those died later.

Not only did she have to deal with the horror of all the dead sheep that day, but she was also a senior in high school with her dues paid one minute and broke the next. The sheep were to have paid for much of her college education at MSU.

Pat had to suffer for years to come from the tragic events. She was forced to borrow lots of money and then also work long hours in the café at Case Hall at MSU for all four years of college. It was a bitter pill to swallow, but somehow my sister did it!

Four years later came a day to remember always, one I will never forget! My sister, Pat drove into the farm driveway with a new car, a new job as a 4-H Youth Agent, and prideful tales of having her own apartment.

I pledged to myself to follow her example that day. Seven years later I equaled her with the same set of goals met. She probably never realized how much she inspired me. I can only thank her now by honoring her with this true story.

The sad events of one day can have a positive effect on another – with faith, effort, and God's grace. I am lucky to have a good and caring sister. In honor of my sister, Dr. Patricia Brown.

Perspectives

Perspectives can change. I recently decided that I had not seen my short straw properly. My years on the farm were trying. During my youth my older brother often bossed me around and roughed me up. I have since talked to several men that had older brothers, and they related that they too had to endure similar treatment.

It is, for me, confounding that parents would allow such treatment to go on. We spent hundreds of hours doing physical labor jobs out away from my parents. Jobs like: picking rocks, loading and unloading hay bales, pitching manure, picking fruits and vegetables, cultivating, etc. In the jobs needing two or more people, I did the harder aspect most every time. I repeatedly tried to inform my parents of the unfairness, but my grievances fell on deaf ears. Then each time my brother discovered I tried to tattletale he would punch me and warn me not to do it again. If I did, I got at least twice as much painful treatment the next time.

That pattern went on for my entire childhood until I was about 15 years old. I punched him in the mouth and knocked a couple teeth loose. You guessed it – my parents' response was why you would punch your nice brother in the face. I told them he had picked on me my entire life, and I got sick of it. I stated that you wouldn't help me so I handled it myself. That slowed things down, but he was stronger and tougher than me.

That treatment by an older brother made me different. I had a younger brother, and I did not pick on him at all. I did have to control and protect him occasionally since my parents made me his keeper a lot. He was 5 years younger than me so I got the nod quite often. I hated being picked on so I didn't pass that on.

I was a teacher for most of my working career, so when the various administrators bothered my students, I was able to stand up for the students when necessary. This was helpful and useful. I would use my influence to protect a student that made a minor error. Going out on the limb when appropriate endeared many students to me. I would cash in those chips later if necessary. It is not a style that I would recommend to a new teacher. You have to have a feel for students and who you are to use that method.

Learning to deal with a difficult person, my brother, as a child, made me stronger and more resilient as an adult. I used to linger on that unfairness from the distant past. I foolishly allowed it to eat at my soul and hurt me. Sometimes we humans are slow learners. It took me until I was 57 years old to let it go and move forward. Only now do I understand that some ill treatment as a youth made me a better teacher and parent.

In 2003, I received a national award for teaching for my 32 years of "exemplary service". The short straw I believed I got as a kid now looks so different. It looks like the longest one now. I learned from my farm life in the past to work hard and never give up. I have always tried to keep my family first and the students at school second.

A balanced lifestyle is easy talk about but harder to live. The only shame was that it took me so many years to wake up to this new realization. I relayed these stories at my men's prayer group. They told me that this may prove to be a big step in my continuing Christian walk. I told the other men that I am so far behind them that I cannot even see them yet. The old saying "live and learn" seems to apply here.

I just dealt with my brother's unexpected death last week at the age of 60 and a memorial service in Florida. I was unexpectedly asked to give a summary of my brother's life and a prayer, which I did. His children were not able to speak, so it was a blessing that I was able to do that task.

God granted me travel mercies and the grace to handle a difficult week. I drove home alone with only a few short breaks. Thirty hours with a loaded van and a side trip to Muskegon to unload. Yes, I have learned that a short straw can grow with God's grace, time and maturity. Events of the past can and do shape your future. It's sensible to glance back and learn from the past, but it is not good to dwell there for too long.

Mushroom Hunting and Looking at Life

Looking for mushrooms and looking for answers about your life can have common ground. Sometimes over the years, the tasty fungi are easier to locate than others. Weather seems to have the greatest effect on size and number of tasty mushrooms that can be found in a given year.

Each person seems to have a list in their mind that they guard dearly of where to locate the highly valued treats; morel mushrooms. When you are trying to get your life together looking in the right places seems to dictate your level of success also. Sometimes the same places that produced excellent results in the past can be a bust the next time around. The seasons of your life change like the seasons of the year. In the past, I earned more money and had less time to enjoy it. Now I have more time, but less money to do some things that could be enjoyable.

It is helpful to remember that when the cement of your life begins to crack and fall apart: What you were is more than what you did for a living. A large part of my personal identity is now lost. Thirty-two years of teaching and three university degrees from MSU means little now. The question now becomes what should your plans be for the days ahead.

Many people today face even more difficult choices. Like mushroom hunting, looking in the same places that were successful in the past do little for you in the future. The best career advice remains the same. Figure out what you enjoy doing and figure out how to earn a living doing it. Something that is legal, moral, helpful to others and something even God would approve of.

Looking in the woods can be good for finding mushrooms – start first by looking under fruit trees. Next, try searching under ash and aspen trees. If the weather is dry, north slopes can be good if it is moist south slopes, of course, heat up earlier and will do better.

Some people have what I call, "good sense." They simply are more in tune with the earth. They can feel which way to go. If you ask them why or how they can sense which way to go or look chances are that either they can't or won't tell you.

I used to allow the students to use a little time if they worked hard and followed directions to look for mushrooms. In 2004 we simply cleaned up on them. We found them by the sack full. Several students that had never found them in the past could scarcely believe their eyes that spring.

In 2005, I went to the same exact place three times and found only a few. The spot could have been easily picked clean since dozens of students were part of the past good fortune. This is a classic example of why a secret spot should be kept secret if possible. It is quite possible that the conditions were simply not favorable for growing mushrooms that year.

In 2006 I found something like 10 mushrooms in the spot. I honestly can't say if it is overly popular or if 2004 was really that great, not to come back again for years and years. I recently heard about a young man and his wife who are going to join a 21st century wagon train. The trip means moving to Florida.

I have been in Florida (to the area where the Marion pioneers are headed) at least 5 times in the last three years. Thousands of new homes are being built where they are headed, so it should work out in that regard.

I wish them God's speed, but it is sad that nice young people from here are now being forced out. I see no good paying jobs and dull future here. Now I wonder to myself how many others will join up and head out somewhere in the very near future. You can even find mushrooms in open fields, but not that often. I pray you will find a few mushrooms and happy hunting this spring.

Bob and Opal

Robert and Opal Johnson were very special people. They are certainly looking down on us from heaven. It was my honor and privilege to be a small part of their lives. The good book, the Bible, was the only guide they used in their lives.

I did not know the featured couple very well until I was 42 years old. My last name is Johnson, but they were my wife's aunt and uncle. My job at the Career Technical Center in Cadillac took me past their home each and every day while traveling to and from work.

They didn't have as much company visiting them during the winter months. They were in their 70's and dashing through the snow was not much fun for them at that point. Since I could stop by without driving out of my way, I made it practice to check-in on them and visit when time allowed. It was always my intention to cheer them up and chit-chat. The problem was that the tables nearly always got turned on me. When I left their humble country home, I was always the one that received the cheering up.

Did you ever have the privilege to hang around lovely people that faced the challenges of aging with faith and grace? I did, and it was a treasure that will be with me always. Complaining was simply not part of who they were or ever talked about. Sure they had medical issues that hampered them, but they did not whine.

I would like to think I could handle the difficulties that linger in the future, but equaling Bob and Opal seems very huge now. The thing is – only with blessings from above could I ever approach being anything like them. Each of them was once in a lifetime type people. When they were in their 80's they would go visit the younger people who were in their 70's at nursing homes and/or were shut-ins. Bob and Opal successfully raised six children. Each of them obtained a college education and had or has an occupation that is beneficial to society: teachers, a ministry, social workers, etc. Helping raise that many children was a big financial burden.

Social security is not a lot of money to live on, so when their adult children realized this, they devised a way to help bridge the gap. A couple of them did a type of reverse mortgage or started buying the house from their parents so Bob and Opal would have a bit of extra money. This keeps the house in the family and helps the immediate situation of having equity but not a lot of cash. This is a graceful way to help your parents while still allowing them to live an independent life.

When you raise caring children God's way, later they likely will want to do what is right for their parents. If you are lucky enough to come across some wonderful people in your life, like Bob and Opal, do not miss the opportunity to get to know them. You'll benefit, and it's what we all should do.

Most people keep rushing around so fast that we could easily miss people gems even when they are in plain sight. I recently met a pleasant fellow up at Autumn Wood in McBain. I was there to visit his roommate, Chet Harwood, who died last week and Merle Robinson was his roommate. It turns out that he is a relative of my wife's, so I asked him if I could visit him. Now on my way home from my men's prayer meeting I have a little extra stop each week. Keep your eyes and heart open and you might be as fortunate as me and meet a few great people that can change your life for the better.

Buster Goes Mad

We had a big, strong German Shepherd dog named Buster back in my early farm days. He was not a dog that you played catch with, or you took to town in the pick-up. However, if you had an angry dairy steer suddenly come after you in the barnyard, then he was the dog you wanted next to you.

These situations came about when you have to dehorn, castrate, or vaccinate cattle. We had hundreds of head of dairy beef. We got them as week old calves and raised them all the way to 1200 pounds market ready steers. We had help when we had to trim the hoofs. Full grown cattle can maim or kill you in an instant. It is best to have a squeeze shoot or tilt shoot to keep yourself reasonably safe. You can use a paralyzer rope lock, but you better do your work fast if you use that method.

We never allowed extra people to be around when serious work with live animals was involved. The reason is that you have to have total concentration and be ready to move the right way in a hurry. It takes years of experience and practice to realize what to do when without instruction.

A sound cattleman is something you have to love to be good at it. Sometimes all goes well, and you have no major problems. Then next day with the same cattle it can be crazy. The weather affects farm animals a lot. People are likewise affected by ill weather more than we all realize.

The dog Buster did little unless he was told. You don't want a loud, pacing dog stirring up the cattle. We never had any trouble with the dog until we were pushing the cattle and a stubborn steer suddenly stopped. Buster rushed up to get the beast moving, and it happened. The steer kicked and got the dog with a direct hit to the head. The dog dropped in a heap; we assumed that it was dead.

My brother, Gary, was crushed. It was his dog for the most part. We were finished working the cattle, and now no one wanted to deal with the downed dog. We quietly headed in to clean up and get ready for supper. My mom asked what was going on. Gary told the sad tale with teary eyes. We ate in silence that night. We went out to bury the dog, but it was up and walking around like a drunk person. The dog sort of recovered after a few weeks.

The dog was out in the milk house drinking from a full milk can. My older sister and brother couldn't get Buster to stop so I grabbed him and threw him back. He lunged at me and bit me directly over the eye. I got more scared than hurt. Although even now I have a scar in my right eyebrow.

Buster had totally changed after the kick in the head. He turned mean. The day after Buster bit me another dog ambled by our house. Buster spotted him, and the big white stray didn't have a chance. Buster tore him to a point of no return. Gary could not call him off.

This even gravely concerned my parents. They did not know how to gracefully handle this situation. My dad was not the person to put down a dog out of control. He simply didn't have the heart for such an undertaking. The vet was called, but Buster did not trust him. The vet tried to shoot the dog, but he missed his mark and only wounded him. Buster took off, and we would see him out in the distance from time to time. Then he was not to be found or seen again. My brother never again liked dogs, and it changed him as well. My brother thought he should now face life with little or no real faith. He often struggled for the better part of his 60 years as a result.

I have been blessed to have a Christian wife and hope to be an upright man with help from God, Jesus and the

Holy Spirit. Why do two people brought up in the same family take different paths?

This is a question for all ages that I can't answer. Can you?

John Deere Hit in the Rear

We were hit in the rear by a speeding car. My brother, Chris, and I were driving a John Deere 420W to the field to bring home the hay rake from a nearby hayfield. We were so far over to the right side of the road that one wheel was completely off the road. The car never hit the brakes at all it simply smashed us directly in the back. The resulting impact sent my brother, Chris, who was riding on the right fender airborne. I grabbed his shirt and changed his flight slightly to the right. This may have saved his life - only God knows the answer to that question. I have saved several people's lives in my lifetime. I went on more than 100 ambulance runs at one point in my life as a volunteer EMT.

Sometimes you can allow your mind to go on auto control, and it simply knows what to do. I was only eleven years old, but I had thousands of hours of operating tractors. I realized Chris would be crushed to death if he could not get out to the side of the tractor's path.

Angels from heaven must have been with us to allow exactly what was needed to occur. So it probably was not me acting on my own at all. I did not realize at that point of my life that miracles can and do happen. I am very fortunate to be alive myself after having blood clots travel through my heart only to become lodged in my lungs not once but twice. The odds of making it through two bilateral pulmonary embolisms in the severe category twice is only three percent. God must have some more work for me, or I would have been called away already.

Back to the crash story, the driver of the car was an older guy, and he smelled like alcohol. He hit his head on the steering wheel or something. It was bleeding a little he had a large goose egg on the forehead. My brother Chris was cut up and bruised all over the place, but he could still walk. The car was smashed pretty well, and the tractor's rear end was split wide open. The engine still ran on the tractor.

The car had lost its radiator, and its coolant spilled on the ground. We all walked to our house only a couple city blocks away. The old fellow tried to look up someone to come and pick him up. I asked him if we should call the police he said no need. His eyesight was so bad he could not read the telephone book at all – I had to look up the number and dial it. The booze smell was really strong inside the house.

I told my parents all this information, but they would not listen. Somehow it must have been my fault. We paid for the tractor repairs and then my parents got the bill for his car. He lied and said I was on the wrong side of the road, and that's why it was my fault. No way that happened. But my parents had our insurance company pay for his car. I never got over being made out to be in the wrong and situations from the past like that still bug me.

I am now and was honest to a fault. It is not easy to be a man of integrity in the 21st century, but I still try. The world seems to have lost much of its notion to be fair, honest and above board. Sad isn't it?

No one was hurt badly thanks be to God. The tractor smash-up is probably more of a nightmare for my brother Chris than me. Flying through the air like the last time in my "Tractors Can Fly" story. I guess I better keep him on the ground for a while. He has taken a couple of good beatings so far already.

The Corn Got Buried

Have you ever gotten in a hurry and regretted it later? It was a hot summer day, and the excitement was in the air. My parents had told us only that morning that we were going on a multiple day road trip. We were to cross the Straits of Mackinac on the car ferry and then proceed all the way around Lake Michigan to Chicago. I had never gone on a vacation trip with my parents before or after that trip. Sad but true – my sister and my brothers went on several trips, but that was it for me. My father passed away in December 2006 so that's the way it has to stay. If you can build fun family memories, please don't let the opportunities get away from you. My wife and I took our children on several travel vacations, and we will always treasure those enjoyable adventures.

We all asked what we needed to do to be able to get started. First, we were to pack-up our clothes and they should include a swimsuit and dress clothes. Second, we were each given our job for the day. Dad said that as soon as we all completed our jobs we could hit the road. My older brother, Gary, was the tractor driver. He was to cultivate the last five acres of corn; we had over 300 acres planted. It would take him about two hours including travel time. He had about lived on the tractor for the past five weeks. The troubles were a brewing big time. Gary left and returned in just over an hour. My dad couldn't believe the job could be done in that quick of a time frame. He drove over to the field where my brother had been working, and he returned as mad as a hatter. In my brother haste to get our trip under way, he ran the tractor in road gear. He later revealed his error in judgment. My dad loaded my mom up front, my sister Pat, my brother Gary, and myself in the back of our pick-up. Dad roared over to the corn field, and the misery began. We had to get the entire field of corn unburied one plant at a time. That is a huge job considering my dad planted the corn at 22,000 plants per acre. So we had to dig it out by hand because at least 50% of the plants could barely even be seen. We each took a row and crawled along pushing the soil away and from the plants. It was sandy so that was helpful. Five hours later we completed the unbelievable task. It is one of the memories burned in your mind that you can't seem to forget. We did head north by about 2 pm from our farm just north of Kalamazoo. Luck was with us we got on the last ferry just before 8 pm. The good Lord was with us less than ten minutes into the Upper Peninsula. We got a motel with a swimming pool. The special for the day at the motel restaurant was pasties and we were as hungry as bears after all the very hot and hard work. The owner must have been part angel; she said we could have 10 large pasties for the price of 5. Plus we got to eat them outside at her picnic table complete, with hot beef gravy and two pitchers of cold lemonade. Heaven it was - I got a cot but it seemed more like a feather bed by now. I was tired and full of tasty food. We stopped the next morning at the Big Spring in the U.P. Wow it was so clear and beautiful! Then we went for a boat tour of the Wisconsin Dells. The weather was great, and the rock cliffs were so pretty. Last we headed down to my aunt's house in Chicago. She had gotten fresh German rye bread and Corned Beef and again we were very hungry. I over ate again and slept soundly. We could see Lake Michigan from her place - what a view! The trip stopped a last time at my Great Aunt Christine's Swedish Bakery. The rolls were flaky and tasty- what a treat. It ended a nice trip that got off to a rough start. May be that beginning helped us to appreciate the sweet ending. God likes to be this way sometimes at least in my life.

Chicken Feathers

Is any smell more branded into one's brain than that of a scalded chicken? Once you've smelled hot, wet feathers, you can never forget it. People who have experienced plucking chicken and burning off pin feathers know exactly what I am talking about. If you don't know- I strongly suggest you avoid this dirty, nasty job.

My younger brother, Chris, has always been a bit of a character. He is the star of this story. We raised chickens of both types: laying hens and stewing hens or fryers. The egg producers were usually White Leg Horns, while the meat types were mostly Vantress. It was often my job to gather the eggs. Four to five-pound hens don't always like to get up and jump off their eggs. Crabby female chickens can and do peck you on occasion. You quickly learn that using your hand to move them off their nests is not such a great idea. Plus rugged, long sleeved clothing is often called for on a working farm. It helps you avoid injuries.

This day we were to butcher about 30 meat birds. My job was to catch the crazy chickens without a crowd pen. That is not so easy. I was about ten years old and good at sports - that helped some I suppose. The long dreaded chicken butchering process was about ready to begin. The water was boiling hot. That meant I was sent scurrying after the frightened chickens. After I had caught them – my dad did what dads do when you're processing chickens. Then mom dipped them into the pot of hot water.

My brother, Chris, was chosen as the chief feather plucker. Slowly, he strolled out of the house, and he was reporting in late for work. At our farm, that was considered a mistake to be avoided at all cost. Although I admit, it was a scene worth remembering. Chris hated the foul smells even more than the rest of us. He approached the chicken coop wearing swim fins and a swim mask. My gosh, it sure was funny, and it made us all laugh out loud.

He quickly ditched the fins, but he actually wore the mask for the entire three-hour chicken cleaning session. It was very difficult to keep a straight face working with a guy plucking chickens with a swim mask on. Yes, the smell always made my stomach churn too. I never did like eating those chickens after that experience. All I ever heard was how good chicken raised on the ground tasted. Food stores now charge you extra for these types of chickens known as free range chickens. I suppose when they eat bugs and worms it might help. But, the memories of the difficult work, the spilled blood, and the various foul smells killed the taste for me.

I do eat chicken now, but I only like wings and breast meat. So, if you ever have to pluck chickens and smell is too much for you put on a swim mask and go to work. The glass does fog up a lot, and the smells might still haunt your nose. But remember what my grandmother Layton said, "There is only one thing better than fun, and that's more fun!" She was right and on the farm happy moments can be few and far between. I hope and pray that you enjoyed a brief smile from the story, or you can remember your own chicken story. If you do I suggest you share it with someone near and dear.

Oh- Rats!

Farms are often the target of rats. History tells us that rats are extremely tough. Rats have been known to jump out of three story buildings, swim for miles in rivers, and they can squeeze through any hole that their head can get through. Rats can eat through concrete walls and wire. You likely already realize that rat's teeth grow continuously like all rodents, so they have to gnaw to wear away their teeth by persistent chewing. Men have never been able to go anywhere on earth without being dogged by rats.

Like most farms in the 1960's, we put our ground feed in 55-gallon barrels with tops to protect it from rats and mice. My brother, Chris, reminded me of this story after I sent him a couple of my recently printed stories. Our ground feed barrels were low on grain - someone would forget to replace the lid on the barrels. My dad loved his barn cats, and he would commonly leave the cover off the feed barrel. That would commonly result in a barrel full of cats that next morning. My dad would simply blindly reach in and lift out the cats. He got out to the barn as usual. My brother liked to drive the pick-up even when he was only about nine years. He pleadingly asked to go get the load of bagged grain. My dad said fine go get the truck. My brother backed up to the barn and Dad, and I started unloading the feed into the barn. Gosh, those bags were heavy, dusty, and awkward. Dad reached into the barrel but came up with a scary surprise, an overstuffed brown rat instead of a cuddly cat. He screamed and threw the fat rat like it was hot metal.

My dad was not so good at being the butt of a joke or funny situation, but we simply couldn't help ourselves. We laughed until we cried. It was just so crazy and weird. The rat ate so much grain it couldn't move. Even after it hit the wall, it could scarcely run. We did learn to use the lids more often after that day. I would carefully peek in before I assumed it was a cat in the bottom after that day.

In the second part of my story, the rats scared my brother, Chris, half to death. For several weeks my parents would head down to Florida each winter. I had headed off to MSU to become trained as a teacher, so that left Chris home alone for quite a while. Chris had no driver's license yet since he was only 14 or 15 years old. Dad had gotten out the big truck - our 3 ton, 20-foot rack grain truck and got 3 or 4 batches of grain all at once. That left Chris' job to transfer it into the pickup and haul it out to the pig feeders.

That process was working well until the last week my parents were to be gone. It was especially cold that winter. Chris was down to the last row of grain bags all the way to the front of the truck. Oddly, he decided he would take the bag in the middle of the last row out first. That set off a rat stampede. The ugly rats panicked when they saw the light and rushed out all at once. My brother was so startled that he fell over backward. The rats proceeded to literally run over the top of him by the dozens. It gave Chris a few nightmares. I bet I still could make him jumpy if I had grain bags up against a wall, pulled one back, and yelled, boo! I know firsthand as I had it happen to me several times around the farm over the years.

Some memories are best left behind. If you were ever around a farm, like me, you probably have a funny rat story or two yourself. May God bless you because if you share a couple of stories, I pray you won't have any bad dreams.

The Bull that Nearly Got Me

The farm animals seen in children's books are not always the reality on a working farm. Especially in the fifties and sixties we still had the 350-pound ram-sheep, the 575-pound boar-hog, and the 1,400-pound dairy Bull. Plus, have you ever handled mature market geese or 20 plus pound Tom turkeys? Believe me, large geese and turkeys are very difficult to herd and catch when you are 7 years old. Frustrating geese bit you in the butt - it's a bite you wouldn't soon forget.

I had various jobs and responsibilities as a farm youth. Some had elements of interest like walking up the dairy cows for afternoon milking. Others included slopping the hogs because pigs always push and shove for position. They always want the most and best food. The bigger stronger pigs knock, the smaller weaker ones out of the way. It's at first fun to watch, but then you get mad at the hogs- the big rude, pigs. You devise schemes to trick the huge guys so the little pigs got a fairer chance. The easiest way is the fake out. You put a small amount in first used pig feeders and a larger amount later at the secondary feeders. By the time the pushy hogs figure out what you did the small hogs have gotten a good meal. This worked for a while then this strategy runs its course; pigs are pretty darn smart, so you have to figure out new plans if time allows. If your hard-nosed dad yells at you get a move on you, have to just do the job fast and plan out your next move when time allows. Doing farm chores is often a stinky proposition. Two reasons: spring and fall involve moisture which means mud when mixed with manure. That adds up to a stinky smell, muddy clothes, and caked up crud on your chore boots. You can't get the odor off your skin or out of your hair without a shower and a change of clothes. I often took 2 or 3 showers per day. My mom shaved us boys heads every month or so. She claimed our wet hair would freeze up and get us sick. We were not alone at school with short hair, but it got us labeled as hay seeds etc. I'll tell you this, though, when football season came around years later, the stuffing generally got knocked out of the city slickers, and the names stopped. "Those rough, tough farm boys" became our new name.

The story of my life, nearly lost, started on a warm summer afternoon. Morris, my dad, told me to take Sox our cow dog, a standard collie, to fetch the cows. It would be milking time soon. This was my favorite job, and I rarely got the opportunity. Gary, my older brother by three years, got the fun jobs. The squirt, me normally, pailed the calves. That meant giving milk, hand-mixed from powdered milk replacement, in pails to young calves in the back of the farm. That was still my job, but I would do that later this day. I started out from out stanchioned dairy barn with about 28 stalls. Cows were trainable when you bring them into the barn, each goes to their memorized place and correct spot. A neck-locking device held them in place so they can be safely milked, at least that's the plan. Our cows were mostly Holsteins, black and white cattle well known to give the most milk. 50 years later that is still the case.

 The story here heads directly down the farm lane. It was a sort of wide two-track with barbed wire fence on each side. You would walk out to the various fields to herd in the cows, in this case for the afternoon milking. Each of our fields had gates and fences all the way around and were 15 to 20 acres. The idea was to keep the cows controlled and confined to a certain pasture. Cows will usually lean on and break down the fences when the rains fail to keep your soil moist and the grass growing well. You are then forced to chase cows all over heck and back. That full story for another day, but we lost twelve head for several weeks and totally lost five head for a good, probably to someone's freezer.

I walked up to the lane gate which I swung open. Our two huge black cherry trees along the way were dead rip, so I quickly grabbed all the fruit my hands could hold. Man, they were good and as sweet as the girlfriend I dreamed about on the way out to the field. It was only about a quarter-mile walk to the pasture where the cows were located. The sun was shining, hundreds of tiger and black swallow tail butterflies fluttered about. What a lovely day, a young farm boy, about 8 years old, a nice dog at your side, warm weather, and an easy job to do. I had reached the field, but I couldn't see any of the cows. I wasn't too worried, there were a couple of hills and valleys out that way. I still had up to a quarter mile to reach the far back corner. They probably would be over the next rise – no luck. One larger hill to go, but something felt odd. My heart was speeding up! How would I be able to round up the cows alone if they somehow had broken down the fence again? Oh darn, this fun and glittering job was rapidly losing its shine. What's going on? The cows are usually scattered about the field. I hadn't seen a single cow yet.

I was now in the middle of our largest field with no cows in sight. Then a young farm lad's worst nightmare had just come true. My enjoyable, relaxing adventure had suddenly turned south. My dad had forgotten to bring in one of the meanest bulls a dairy farm had seen in our parts for many years. He was dealing with the Milk Inspector's second visit. We had white washed the entire barn that day. It is a terrible, dusty task. You splash smelly white powder on every floor, wall, and ceiling in the entire barn. You get totally covered with the stuff, there is no way to avoid it.

I tried heading slowly out of the field. The bull spotted me. I was dead meat! He charged – I literally ran for my life. I was running as fast as I could. After only a short distance I knew I wasn't going to be fast enough. If you ever watch bull running on TV, you'll never see a kid out in the ring with the bulls. But that was my situation. I raced past the only tree in the field, no help as the first limbs were too high to reach. I was quickly losing the race. The mean, nasty bull was now so close I could hear him breathing. No way I could reach the outside fence in time. Plus, how could I ever jump over the fence – fast enough to keep from being crushed to death. I was about to be killed. God saved me. I looked back for the last time.

Suddenly, from out of nowhere, Sox our dog, crashed into the bull's neck. She latched on as tight as she could. She was trampled in an instant, but it caused the raging bull to stumble briefly. That's the instant I needed to reach the edge of the field. The 48-inch fence was dead ahead. I was out of time and luck. A new barbed-wire fence and now was my moment. I jumped for all I was worth. I soared high and somehow cleared the wire. Only then did I see the raspberry patch directly under me. It was too late – direct hit. I was instantly shredded by hundreds of barbs. Blood poured out from places you can't imagine and don't want to. The bull hit the fence and tore several steel posts down. I tried scrambling to my feet for a second but I was so caught up in briers they threw me down hard. I crawled out as quickly as possible. I was still in grave danger.

The mad bull shook its massive head and charged again and again. The fence tightened and sang, but held. God was still with me because the bull's nose ring got wrapped into the wire and the bull was now done, at least for a while. I sprinted toward the house. My legs were bleeding like all get out. I knew that it wasn't that serious.

I had crashed into the briers once before in the winter while sledding down some crazy steep hills.

I made it to the barn when Dad saw me from a distance and at first, he started to get mad. But I blurted out that the bull had almost got me! He only then realized his near fatal error. He excitedly asked if I was badly hurt – I said no. I'd be fine. I nervously yelled that the bull was still caught in the fence. He was held by his nose ring. You better get help, he's going crazy. Dad quickly went into the house and called my uncle Gordon. He came right over and brought a rope with a strong clip to snap onto the bull's nose ring. He was totally worn out by then. They tied him to the back of a tractor and dragged him up the lane, home to his bullpen. Phyllis, my mother, stripped off my bloody clothes and cleaned me up. I somehow had lived through another day thanks to a brave dog and leaping power beyond what I should have been capable of. The big guy in the sky allowed me to nearly fly over that tall fence for some unknown reason! My dog limped home later. I hugged her repeatedly, and mom gave her some nice soup bones. We all petted her for quite a while that night and for several weeks to follow. Dad milked the cows, and my uncle stayed and helped. I got the calves fed.

Then we farmers came home from the barn. My mom was in the kitchen making beef gravy to go with our supper. The wild events of the day were rehashed. Uncle Gordon told us the story about his daughter being nearly eaten alive by his pigs when she was thrown from her horse in the swine lot. This is a good story for another day. The bull was hauled away in a few days. My dad told us all that he had also been attacked by the bull. I was plagued with a lot of scary dreams for a while, but they went away with time.

Old School Bike Riding

The neighborhood boys and I literally rode the tires and wheels right off our bikes. When I was between 8 to 14 years old, we would commonly ride our one-speed bikes 30 to 50 miles on a normal Sunday. Swimming was the prime activity, and fishing was a distant second.

We started peddling in March and we cranked until early October. As soon as you left the yard there were no parents to boss you around. Freedom was yours on a bike with your own places to go and things to see. We knew every coasting hill within 25 miles and nearly all houses with mean dogs lurking about. We all lived near Cooper Center, in Kalamazoo County, Michigan. Bike rides evolved as we went. One of us would start out and pick up the others along the way. It was not uncommon to meet the clan partly assembled halfway around the pick-up points.

Girls didn't ride with us very often. They held us up and had trouble with the stopping-to-pee issues that came up with daylong rides. A couple of girls that were tomboy types would occasionally join us. They would want to stop at every swimming hole for a dip, an apparent alternative more modest way to pee. Some of my girl first cousins rode with us guys a few times. They stopped most anywhere if need be. They were no problem and they would catch up. The guys thought they were cute and fun.

We always wore swim suites for underwear during the summer months. The nearest swimming hole was about three miles away. It took us about 15 minutes to get there. The closest swimming hole was called Frost's Pond. We were not always welcome there. It was fenced in and it had a very tall water slide. I would guess it to be about thirty feet tall.

The owners believed themselves special and somewhat better than us clod busters. The Frost's had wheeled sleds that sped down the slide at wild crazy speeds. You would ride down and skim across the water for 25 feet or more. It was great fun plus they had a nice raft out in the deep water. The place got too popular in time and drunks started to show-up by the car loads. That was the end of years of great times of the Cooper Coolies, as we called ourselves.

Swimming hole cool-offs from then on were history. You couldn't blame the owners. Someone broke in while drinking, fell off the slide, got hurt, and tried to sue. The slide had to be torn down and the pond was actually drained. It makes me sick to think how people that lack respect can ruin a good thing for respectful people like us honest farm kids.

We went to the next pond on the same stream farther down. Danny, my friend, lived there and we never told a soul where we went swimming after the bad boys took over and wrecked our best spot. It wasn't much fun without the slide and raft. The swimming trips got fewer and fewer after things went south.

We rode bikes to go fishing also but we found it hard to make it to the lake with your bait and pole. Then if fishing was good getting a bunch of fish home and cleaned was nearly impossible. We had our favorite routes they usually involved the longest coasting hills. The downhill was a rush but it also meant you had to face a long difficult uphill climb sometime on the return trip.

We didn't need to carry water in the 60s. If you got thirsty you stopped by most anyone's dog-less house and turned on the hose. Very few people would care, giving only an occasional, "be sure to shut the hose off." Several people must have been pleased to see us exercising, out of the house, and having fun. It was not uncommon to be offered a bottle of pop if the lady of the house was home.

Kalamazoo had its own hometown soda bottling plant, Os's. They specialized in interesting flavors including: lime, black cherry, orange, and grape to name a few. It was sold by the case of 24 only in 10-ounce bottles. Two dollars per case if you brought the bottles back in good condition.

Riding bikes was an adventure and generally great fun. I only wish kids today could enjoy it and parents would be able to trust people to leave their kids alone. The good old days were better for keeping kids healthier and active. I wore out three bikes in my day and still smile when I remember the bike riding days. Forty years later I still like to ride bikes. It is enjoyable to ride the six miles to town and back. God helps us all enjoy life and a nice breeze in the face sure can make you feel good.

Hay Stories

Baling hay was a hot, dusty, and difficult work in the 1960's. The bales weighed 60-85 pounds and we used string or twine. It was not that uncommon for our farm to bale 50,000 between hay and straw. We owned four sesquicentennial farms and 300 acres of land. Hay was our main cash crop; we used six hay wagons. It wasn't uncommon for us to cut hay in the rain. Some years we handled up to 200 acres of hay with three cuttings, yielding 600 acres of cuttings. That is a bunch of cuttings using only a seven-foot sickle bar mover and nine-foot steel rake.

I raked hay when I was 7 years old or as soon as I could reach the clutch pedal. My dad told me to stay in second gear which I did for a couple rounds, then I shifted up to third gear. He knew if I had enough confidence to go faster I would be safe and fine.

You face trials all the time on a farm. It is part of life there. The choices are to do exactly as you're told or to be a leader and show you have guts. Sometimes you were punished and sometimes the reward was silence. Seldom were you praised; it was simply what was expected of you.

I believe it was an odd system. It helped me later when I was a teacher. I never played that card with students it's simply too confusing. Trying to continuously guess what you should do is too stressful and unfair. Each person reviews their past and harvested the grains of wisdom wherever they can be found. Until I started writing these stories for the newspaper I had not understood some of the methods for my madness. I used these lessons to help my wife and me to successfully raise our three children. Praise be to God with his help all things are possible. Being fair and consistent as a parent or teacher with your children and students was, and still is, the best personal advice I can give you. It is a gift that keeps on giving. You'll have much less difficulty if you use these principles.

    I rode on top of the stacked bales some 15 feet off the ground that day. We were rather poor, so my dad made up his own wagon running gear. It had a swinging straight axle. The problem is when the wagon is turned sharply the inside corner is overloaded; as a result, the corner dips down, the load shifts and you can tumble to the ground. That's the first problem when I hit the ground and had the wind knocked out of me. The second problem was all the hay fell off the wagon, landing on top of me. I was literally buried alive under thousands of pounds of hay. I couldn't see a thing, move a muscle, or breathe. My all-star cousin, Duane, quickly dug me out and saved my life. It was a moment that scares me to this day. Helplessness is a bad feeling; one you can't easily get past. I couldn't work for a few days I was severely beat up and sore. My dad asked me why I was so stupid to sit on top of the load, but there was no other place to sit. There were times when I was a kid and became angry toward my dad, and that was one of them. However, that crappy wagon was parked for good. Getting hurt and then being yelled at is tough stuff for a young child to endure. My dad never hugged or kissed me, but few men of the WWII generation ever showed much love toward others. The stress of war probably hurt them more than they ever realized.

I later played high school football, and our coach would yell at us for no good reason at times. Many athletes on my team suffered a lot from that type of ill treatment, but it had little effect on me. Why, because I had been the victim of that situation many times over the years. I learned to ignore bad treatment most times.

Guys in college quit the fraternity during hell week also, but again although I disliked that type of treatment I could tolerate it for short periods. I never messed with pledges when I became an active fraternity member.

Harsh lessons can be used for good, but not everyone develops the resilience to deal with the difficult situations life gives you in a positive manner. The Holy Spirit helps me daily, and I realize I can't handle all things alone. Peace be with you. Keep the faith and may God bless you. Hard work and working your way through trials makes us all better people if we have a positive attitude.

Beaver Dam Things

Have you ever fought with a beaver? If you have, you'll find them to be very determined and stubborn. We had dozens of the sturdy rodents munch up thousands of our aspen trees.

My wife was born and raised around here. The very thought of the destruction got her dander up. It had little to no effect on me. My students were always taught that each ecosystem has a certain carrying capacity. This means beaver will, in due time, stop eating and cutting down your trees. The neighbors to the south that have forty acres said they were appalled and concerned. They asked for my advice and wondered what should be done. So I told them to harvest the poplar trees as soon as possible. A few days later several pulp trucks, a grapple skidder, and a sawhead feller-buncher took to their rolling hills. The vast majority of the pulp-sized trees were removed by the hundreds in short order. In two days the job was complete, and a check for over $10,000 was received by my neighbors. Plus, they actually thanked me for my honest, straight-forward advice.

Our side of the pond had been harvested a few years before that point in time by the previous owners. So few trees were actually large enough to be harvested as pulpwood on our side of the pond. My kids and I decided we would challenge the mad rodents. My three kids, Eric, Amy, Alex and I plus my nephew, Christopher, took off for our small creek and large beaver pond. We each wore our grubby clothes and carried lots of hand tools. We had hoes, rakes, corn rake-hoes, shovels, and a couple of axes. The beaver had created several smaller dams in the stream. We were determined to rip them down. It turns out that nature's engineers are extremely clever and wise. You have to rip and pull the limbs out of the strongly woven dam one piece at a time. I had a lot of practice dismantling these soil laden and leafy piles of woven, tensioned tree limbs. The rushing water and mushy stream bottoms are hard to stand still in. A sudden current is created as the direct result of removing and dismantling beaver dam materials.

This was the first time I included my children in the actual efforts. The water was only a few feet deep. This made the project more like a live puzzle and a reasonably safe supervised activity. You can explain all you like, but when you go into the cold, slippery water, the true reality starts to sink in. Eric sloshed in first as I warned him of the difficulties that lingered. He had a good start and waded toward the first short dam with no problems. He started with a hoe and pulling down the top limbs and was making slow progress.

The others ventured in to help as they decided to work together and give a giant pull all at once. They counted to three, tugged hard and busted loose a huge section. That's nice, but the resulting current nearly washed them all away downstream. They were scared only for a few seconds - then the laughter rang out.

The action continued for over an hour as they chopped, pried, pushed and tore those three smaller dams down in the end. They were muddy, soggy, and worn out. It was one of those days when I was wise enough to stay back and enjoy the kids having a great time just being kids. I am sure the size of the dams will grow in size as the years pass but a day of good fun is rare.

The kids ate twice the goulash they normally ate that day and lots of watermelon as well. Time to watch kids grow in God's way is surely a special gift. One more year and we'll have three MSU graduates. Wow, time flies.

Fruits and the Human Spirit

Picking raspberries and strawberries are often like life. You do your best to locate all the sweet fruits and the first time down the patch. When you look at the same row from a different angle on the second trip through you almost can't believe all the wonderful berries you missed. Life is often the same way. Seeing things fresh in a different light can bring you a lot of great fruits.

My family tried about every possible way to make money on our farm when I was young. We lived on a very busy paved road so my mom decided raising and selling strawberries would be just the ticket.

Several varieties were selected and planted in the early fall. All berries selected had different maturities. We had lots of good cattle and chicken manure and rich soil. It had been a great spring, and the plants were loaded. It usually takes longer, but God's grace was with us. We sold lots of strawberries for the first couple of weeks.

Then we suffered a disastrous event – the neighbor's dairy herd trampled the entire patch. Most of the plants were ripped apart with the vast majority of the berries crushed.

The cattle got loose a couple more times and all the hand planting, weeding, and picking were lost. The only compensation we got from the neighbors responsible was a, "It won't happen again". My parents were so disgusted that they actually bought a farm in a different location some five miles away.

When your hopes and dreams are torn apart, you can whine and mope, but it really doesn't do anyone any good. People that are most progressive and successful learn that you need to continuously reinvent yourself. This is not a natural process for the majority of humans. The reason to push yourself through these walls and barriers to success is that technology changes quickly. If you remain as you were you'll stay where you are, and that will leave you behind in a short amount of time.

Other people that are able to rapidly change with the times can pass you by. If you try to take too many shortcuts or walk over others in the process of career building, you can trip yourself up in the process. It can be a trail you are not prepared to tackle. If that is the case, it is your responsibility to work your way through, past, or around the situation.

The correct attitude is to look at it as an opportunity for growth and maturity. You will meet many people in your lifetime that are either unwilling or unable to refine themselves, their talents or their abilities.

If I use myself as an example, I am most generally direct and straight forward. That characteristic normally served me well over the years. However, bluntness and direct honesty can be difficult for some people to handle. This is especially true for people that believe they always have the best answer to a challenging situation.

I learned over the years to do better at not throwing in my two cents. It builds people up to be stronger long-term if they can learn for themselves if the time and cost are not too great; stand and stay back. It is hard to do, but it is better for your children. The Bible tells us to build up your children that way for the best results.

I picked several quarts of raspberries at some great peoples' house the other day – the Fredins. I was reminded how lovely a nice conversation can be when your hands are busy doing useful tasks. Being around fine Christian people is good for my soul. Plus, I got my wife involved later turning it into some very tasty freezer jam using lower sugar Sure-Jel. When we work together, we all win. It's too bad people trying to run the country can't figure that out, it sure would make a welcome change.

We raised raspberries at my parent's farm both red and black. My gosh, it takes a long time to pick those seedy black ones, and mosquitoes love to hang out in them. In the 1980s we started raising ever-bearing varieties. You prune them each fall by mowing them off, and that suited my dad who didn't like to prune. My mom dragged my dad into many different jobs and situations over the years. But I guess it came out pretty good for him and my mom. They were able to spend six months a year for thirty years enjoying the warm and agreeable winters of Florida, then the other half of the year, for nearly twenty years, was spent at a nice lake in southern Michigan.

Oh yes, they like all farmers will tell you about hard they work or worked. It can be true, but how many of us will ever live the life my parents lived in their later years? They did build or develop a house large enough to have a rental or two, so it wasn't a free lunch.

God gives to those willing to put forth the effort needed to get ahead in life. I could probably do like my parents and move to Florida, but I may find a quieter place somewhere.

Squirrel Hunting

The cool weather reminded me of another story about a great fall activity. My Grandfather Jack Layton and I each loved the cool, crisp, and beautiful days of fall. Hunting squirrels is a relaxing and enjoyable way to spend a sunny afternoon. You basically sit quietly in a woods containing lots of oak trees. If some fox or gray squirrels bother you enough, you might try a shot at one of them.

The experience of smelling fallen leaves and walking among the lovely leaves is wonderful. The full pallet of beautiful fall colors remaining on the trees is one of God's prettiest bouquets.

It seemed odd at the time that when we sat out there together leaning against those tall and mighty trees that grandpa would nap. Can you think of a better place to rest and enjoy a beautiful fall day?

We would often be suddenly brought back to the possibility of getting a squirrel when the chattering started. The mocking of squirrels would sort of make fun of us or was it just them telling us to go home? One way or another we would wake up as the result of the sudden noise.

My grandpa would act like he was awake the whole time. He actually got a couple of them a few times. I always went along with his secret because I really enjoyed the time just being able to go along with him.

Jack Layton was known to be easily irritated and rather crabby. I learned at an early age not to cross him. If he said to leave his things alone, that's what I did.

Sometimes you can learn that people have a reason why they are the way they are. My grandpa was extremely bright but his family either couldn't or wouldn't help him reach his dreams. He wanted to go to college, but they basically didn't support his dreams. He had to work at a paper factory in Kalamazoo to support his family. He generally hated working there, but it paid better than most other jobs. Then, later in his life, he fell off the top of bleacher stands at a race car track, during construction and became a diabetic as a result. We can all say we wouldn't become bitter but are you sure? I say there is no way one can be sure how we will react to difficult trials.

It was enjoyable for me to learn whatever good things I could from my grandpa. He could fix almost anything. I would stand quietly and watch him work. People seem to be too willing in present times to ditch anyone that has different values than themselves. That is a troubling reality because as the world continues to shrink, discernment and strong people skills are more - not less - necessary.

Yes, you can learn to see good in most people if you look hard enough. I did that with my grandpa, and he taught me a lot.

Fall will soon be here. Get out there and enjoy it. God willing you'll smile a lot and have a great fall.

Harvest Time

Nothing compares to the joy of a bountiful harvest time on a farm. Filling the hay loft, wheat bins, corn cribs, canning jars, and the freezer with meat and vegetables was a rewarding and proud event. All the long hours of tilling, planting, baling, combining, raking, dragging, disking, cultivating, weeding, and picking seemed to make sense at last.

Farmers are an odd lot. Optimism is the motto of farmers who have an inclination to anticipate the best possible outcome of actions. The dictionary gave me this definition, and it is certainly a good way to denote how a farmer thinks.

My main job was the hauling and unloading of harvested materials. It was a dawn to dusk and beyond race. It was common to go all night if we had the storage room.

My family seemed to have an extra gear when the harvest was going full blast. That was very enjoyable for me because the silly stuff, like arguing, seemed to be put aside each fall. As I recall past autumns with all their beauty, surely our positive family teamwork added to this most wonderful time of year.

You could handle the needed, difficult physical labor easily in the cooler weather. Shoveling load after load of ear corn off a flatbed wagon was one job I could have skipped without feeling bad. My dad built a homemade gravity box wagon; it was not great, but it sure beat handling corn one scoop at a time. We later got a self-propelled combine and went to shelled corn. That was easier because we acquired an auger and it cut down on at least half the hand-work. We then got a 300-bushel flatbed truck and a 300-bushel straight truck with a dump box.

That sure was exciting, especially when you hauled it down to the grain elevator. You could empty the truck with a quick sweep out with a broom. That was needed because when you are harvesting four rows at a time instead of two, you have a lot of grain to remove to keep the very expensive diesel powered combine moving. You can't make or save money if it is sitting waiting to unload.

We also added a gravity box wagon and to our collection of wagons. Three in all, with added side racks, so empty at the beginning of the day we could hold 1,200 bushels. That sounds good, but that only gets you to lunch time. So the wild scramble to unload ASAP starts with the first 300-bushel truckload.

It was a fun rush to see how fast you could get to town and unload, usually only 5 miles away, and get back in 30 minutes. I would go into the elevator late in the evening if necessary but if I couldn't unload the grain on the truck that was a problem. When that happened, I would go in early the next morning so I might be first in line. Dad would always be glad to see that I had already left the house by 6 am or a little before. The grain elevator opened at 7 am during harvest season. The early arrivals and hustling attitude paid-off later when I needed a job in the summer to earn money for college. The grain elevator owners hired me for two summers at good pay.

God blessed me then and later with a nice wife and family. That is a harvest no one can beat.

Yes, I loved the thrill of harvest and the colors of a lovely fall. I hope you each have a good story to share with your family. It is always later than you think - so share important memories with your family while you still are able. Life is good, and fall is beautiful.

An Afternoon to Remember

Gifts can take many forms. My sons, Eric and Alex, and myself, Dale, each received a wonderful and unexpected present last summer.

My uncle, Norris J. Layton, shared a long string of WWII stories with us. He is 90 years old, and he must have felt the need to share these superlative and stunning experiences.

We took him to lunch at a nice place on Torch Lake. There was no plan or agenda that day. We all just wanted to enjoy a beautiful afternoon. That certainly happened, but it was an afternoon none of us, that had the privilege to experience, will ever forget.

Can you in your wildest dreams imagine being behind enemy lines during WWII in Germany, knowing one slight slip of the tongue could mean your life? That's exactly where my uncle was located. Is it any wonder that my uncle guarded us for most of his lifetime from these ugly and horrible memories?

If you ever had any doubts that these horrendous and dreadful events were real and actually occurred, the testimonial we heard – I assure you – would cancel any doubts and likely result in a number of nightmares.

My uncle actually saw hundreds of expired Germans. These dead were the direct result of experiments done on their own people. The people were told to do difficult, strenuous work with little food and rest.

These tests were setup to see which humans could withstand the most stress for the future development of the master race under Hitler's orders.

This is only my guess but is seems to have merit. My uncle was able to speak German as he heard and spoke it some as a child. His mother, her brothers, sisters, and many members of his family used it at home. Plus, he studied German at Western Michigan University as part of his teacher preparation program.

Living behind enemy lines during a world war must have been like living inside a hot pressure cooker. I doubt anyone can put aside seeing people die and being mistreated to the point of death. My uncle's solid use of German was a huge headache as the war wound down. He had the worse job I have ever heard of in my lifetime.

His job as a Captain in the U.S. Army was to dispose of thousands of human bodies left unburied. I will skip this part as it was extremely disturbing to hear these details. I wish I could have recorded these soul-rocking stories.

My sons and I could not talk during our car trip on the way home. We simply reflected and prayed in silence that this sick and sad treatment of human beings will never be repeated!

I hope this story helps us all remember what the military did and still is doing to protect our freedoms.

Thanks be to God that our country stood-up and took on the crazy Germans and Japanese and defeated them both in turn. Thanks go out to my uncle for sharing from his heart the real and important stories that needed to be told and shared with his family.

Tractor on the Edge

Things can and do happen quickly when you operate tractors on a farm. This summer day I was baling wheat straw stubble at the Kalamazoo Nature Center. My father was the farm manager there. I was using a small bale machine as nobody had the large round bale rollers used today that can reach over six feet tall in diameter. My tractor that day was hand clutch Case DC, a 45 horsepower model, with a new Massey-Ferguson baler on the back.

It was about four o'clock in the afternoon, and I had been running the baler since about ten in the morning. The counter had recorded 1700 bales. It was mid-July, and I remember we charged 10 cents per bale so my dad was going to be rather happy. It was the last round on the field.

I had started raking the fields at seven in the morning. The heat, sun, and dust had taken its toll on me. I was only 13 years, but I made a rookie mistake that day. You should always reverse your motion on the last round and travel counter-clockwise on the outside round. That keeps the tractor toward the inside of a field where it's safer. I knew better but tried to avoid walking around a 20-acre field having to throw off all the bales on the inner round by hand. So, off I went taking the short cut.

God or as least a guardian angel or two must have been with me that afternoon. I had not gone 100 yards when the tractor started sliding down a thirty-foot cliff. I quickly shut-off the tractor and was about to jump. Then I jumped over the wheel on the up hillside and landed on the rim. Somehow that was just enough weight to keep the tractor from rolling down the cliff.

Then the situation got interesting. I couldn't leave. I stood on that rim waiting for someone to come looking for me. Dad was working at the other farm and would not be coming for a long time. I tried to move but when I tried to get off the tractor started to tilt. So there I stood in a huge pickle not able to leave. One hour, then two, and three – I was getting very scared. Then I got a bad leg cramp. My eyes were watering, and I was extremely stressed.

Finally, Dad came looking for me. He yelled at me, "What the heck are you doing over there on the tractor rim?" Then he began to realize the emergency situation at hand. He said, "Stay still - I'll go get the bigger tractor, and we'll chain it up to get you out of there." He had to go home and get the tractor first as he had the pick-up truck. He said he would be right back. That took another half-hour or so, but he came with a Case 800B, a 12,000 pound plus tractor. We chained the tractors together, and I safely backed the tractor and baler off the cliff edge. I had to do the dangerous job, but we saved the tractor and the new baler. I wasn't asked how I was or if I was ok. Dad got after me, and I deserved it. I used poor judgment. I could have been killed, but God saved me.

I was then told to walk the field and throw off the bales. Then I finished baling the last round, going around the proper way. I went home with the tractor and baler and got home at 9 pm. I spent fifteen long hours working that day. That's tough stuff for a kid.

Many a time after that day the Lord kept me safe. Later after college at MSU, I went to Belize, C.A. where I served and trained Peace Corp volunteers. There I had people I didn't even know try to kill me. Well, I'll save that for another day. Peace be with you thanks for reading my story. I hope you enjoyed it!

Grandma's Visit Rules

Lida Caroline Layton was what people of the older times called, "A good egg!" She was good-natured and fun to be around. It was difficult for anyone to see her mad. Lida was the oldest of nine children; as a result, she was more or less a mother to her brothers and sisters at an early age. It probably helped her be such a good grandmother and fun loving person. Living through the Great Depression as an adult probably gave her a more balanced perspective and a "things-seem-pretty-good-to-me" attitude.

All seven of us grandkids got a turn to have the privilege of staying at Grandma and Grandpa Layton's house. She had one rule- that being only one grandchild at a time allowed at her house. That is what helped make the time spent there so special. That was her way of doing things at her house. She had a saying on the wall, "this is my house, and I'll do as I darn well please." My mom thought she was selfish for it. All seven of us grandchildren loved it. You knew when it was your turn it was going to be special. First, no brother or sisters to argue with. Second, no one there picking on you or interrupting the activity. Third, you had grandma or grandpa to yourself with all the lovely experiences that entailed.

If you have grandchildren, you might want to consider using this system or method. It is less stressful for the older person, it is quieter, and it might keep you from being a cheap babysitter for your kids. This is less valuable if your kids are several states away. Why not have one at a time for a couple of weeks. This makes the visit a special treat for you and the child. If you do all the work and driving, then it tells you things. Mainly, you may not be that valuable or appreciated by your own kids.

You can make the pick-up part of another natural trip for example on your way to visiting your brothers, sisters, or other friends. This is assuming now that those visits are also not just a one-way trip with you doing all the traveling and paying all the costs. A one-way street is a lonely one over time and is not a good trip. A reasonable balance is the ideal mix you visit them then they visit you. Some people seem to always want to play the- I am so busy card. Remember the busiest of people make time for important things and others. I meet frequently with a couple of millionaires, several busy business owners, and just plain common people like myself. Does this make me special-no not at all. It tells you that these people care about other people and events beyond themselves.

My opinion presently points more often to people in the twenty-first century turning towards being self-centered. They rush home, watch "reality TV," play computer games, constantly watch satellite TV, surf the net, and wonder why their kids are poor readers, impolite, and inconsiderate. These activities should be limited if not avoided. You should never allow your kids to have computer or TV in their rooms. It is like inviting strangers to stay overnight in your house without even knowing who they are.

Old sayings hold strong yet like, "you have to be a friend to have a friend." People claiming to say or believe they are too busy may lack character or the ability to say "no."

Make time for your grandchildren because they are a gift that not everyone has or can get. This is the way I see the issue of why you should consider only allowing one kid at a time to be with their grandparents. I truly loved my special time as the only superstar with my grandma. She was great. I pray I can be a little like she was for me; kind and wonderful to be around. I now have several grandchildren – I consider it a blessing from God. Go bake some cookies and have fun with those that need your time and love.

Deer Hunting in Southern Michigan

The deer are bigger, and the guns are not able to shoot as far. When I was younger, I commonly would see bucks of ten points and more. This is not bragging. There is simply a greater density of corn and beans and less swamp land and woods. The deer face milder winters and longer summers. South of M-57 you have to use a shotgun or muzzle loader during the firearms season.

My dad would not allow us to hunt off the combine or picker wagons like many other farmers and their families allowed. Also, we had so much work to do, and we all played high school sports. The weekends were spent doing farm work, and I did not have a gun to use either. It was sure hard to hear the other farm kids brag about the big deer they got when you had no chance at all. My dad loved to see the big deer even though he complained constantly about the destruction the deer did to our crops. It is my experience that griping is a way of life for many farmers. They'll tell you how things are tough but they drove to town with a new pick-up. Then they get the biggest most expensive breakfast as if they have no food at home. Farmers are generally quite a group of characters. It is just plain funny to think about now! My family had 300 acres and sold it all for over one million dollars. I lived my entire youth as a poor person. Now my mom has things good, a nice house on a channel in Florida and a condo at Grand Haven. It is, however, difficult for newly widowed farm wife with resources to now be generous. Money was scarce when I was young; now my mom acts like things are still that way in many respects. Old ways are difficult to change. I would like to go to Florida some in the winters but with kids still in college, that is simply not possible. Plus, my wife is not ready to retire, and I will never have the money my parents made with fifty years of owning large amounts of land. I do not regret not being rich in money because there are better ways to be rich. My wife, mother-in law, my sons, and I just shared a nice Halloween Birthday party for my son Eric this week in Lansing. How much is a lovely day with your family who are all active and loving Christians worth? I am very blessed and I try to never forget it. So if you have a chance to deer hunt at a farm in southern Michigan I strongly suggest you go give it a shot. The deer are bigger, it's not as cold, you'll see more deer, and less people while hunting. Get out there have a great time being out-of-doors and getting some fresh country air.

Thanksgiving Thoughts

"The good things that we've got are for many just a dream," as sung in a Christian song by female singer Evie. It can be difficult at times to be thankful for the many blessings most of us have. This is the time of year that we are to review our lives and make the proper adjustments. Looking at ourselves and families in regards to finances, faith, and our futures can be challenging. You can skip this process, but it can be a mistake - because if you're dropping deeper into a hole, you can get buried and get in over your head. I took an intense training program to be better able to help people wanting assistance with their finances through Crown Financial Ministries. If you listen to radio stations, like Northern Christian Radio, you can hear the program, "Money Matters;" they are sponsored by Crown. I am now a "Money Map Coach!" I taught a class this year so those involved would be better able to follow the basics and learn to be better at budgeting. If you are interested, I'll try to get you on a path moving toward debt free living. Eight percent of all families in the U.S. now spend more money than they make and are going deeper in debt by about $500 per month. Looking at things in your future is another good exercise this time of year. It can also be helpful to glance back at your past to determine if you made mistakes that you should avoid if given a second chance. If you're planning to have a nice Thanksgiving meal with family or friends, it might be enjoyable to ask each person gathered to mention one thing they are thankful for before the meal. This can be fun and revealing. It is best to not push those gathered if they seem uncomfortable with this exercise. Some family members not in a proper frame of mind can find this too stressful.

It can be a good move to attend a nice Bible believing church this time of year. Even if you're not a regular, it can be a good place to meet new friends and rekindle old friendships. Another bonus is worship songs sung in today's services are generally uplifting and upbeat. The verbal message you are likely to hear could renew your spirits. A good way to start out the day at our house would be to see my son, Alex, and myself out deer hunting. One year he told me he was going out and if I hear a shot come and help him field dress the buck he was going to get. He made me laugh as he did not even dress warmly and sure enough he got a nice buck. So have a very nice day this Thanksgiving and try your best to enjoy yourself and the day.

The Winter Fun and the Wild Toboggan Ride

Riding a toboggan on fresh deep snow is great fun. Most of my younger years were spent living in the rolling hills of western Michigan. We had dozens of good sliding hills. It was good exercise and honest fun to ride down speedy hills. When I was a kid, we would often run up the hill after going down. How many kids today would be healthy and ambitious enough to even think of going outside to go sliding? Maybe I am just being negative, but I see a lot of heavy kids that probably couldn't even make it up the hill more than a couple of time. The hard work I was required to do made us country kids tough, especially farm boys like me.

Another good time was shoveling snow off the pond so we could play broom hockey. We would work for an hour to play for an hour. Some years we would have ice skating parties on one of our many ponds. Building a nice campfire to keep warm and roast some hotdogs or marshmallows was a very special treat for us all. It was not uncommon for us to put gallons of cocoa into a ten-gallon milk can and pull it out to the skating party. We sat close to the fire so it would keep us warm. Sometimes if the weather wasn't bad someone would play a guitar, and most of us would sing along. Things that were common fun then are uncommon fun now.

Our best pond was in a perfect location. It was close to the road, but not too close, about seventy yards away. This allowed parents to drop off their kids, and they could see that it was safe and supervised. Later, if they were so inclined, they could pass by and see that their kids were still there and ok. A nice bonus was that a pretty good hill that could be used for sliding was on one side. This occasionally created a collision between sliders and ice skaters. Some bad boys would try to time their sled ride so a cute girl would fall on top of them down on the pond. Of course, I wasn't one of those fellows. It was common to have kids bring their new Christmas sleds, saucers, or skates so they could try them out. We had both planned and unplanned parties. Adults driving by with no kids or empty nesters would come down and just watch us kids enjoying some good clean fun. We knew the neighbors for miles around in those days. Things were different in the sixties in some ways better some ways not so great.

Oh yes, the wild, dangerous toboggan story. My older sister, Pat, wanted to take a ride on the freshly waxed toboggan. That's when a couple of issues she hadn't planned on that both got her on a trip down the hill. First, the snow had a crust of ice on top. We had to work hard to bust through it with three of us kids riding down together. Once we had a groove, it was fast and fun. Second, Pat got a huge surprise when she decided to take a solo run to start a new run on the steepest hill. She did not cut through the crust. She rode on top of the crust. And as if that weren't bad enough a runaway toboggan with no way to steer - now add on a two hundred and fifty-pound football player. Ruddy O' Boyle, a distant neighbor boy who never came over before, came running from out of nowhere like a crazy man and jumped on the back of her speeding toboggan. All the extra weight created what appeared to be sub-light speed. Pat was headed for a tree, and she had to intentionally crash before that happened, if possible. All you can do when you're the driver is pull as hard as you can and lean one way or the other. She leaned for all she was worth, the toboggan cut into the crust, but the sudden braking sent her down the hill head first, ahead of the toboggan. Pat surfed on top of the icy surface for a short distance then just as suddenly she cut through. The ice sliced into her face. The sight of blood on snow still makes me cringe when I recalled the scene. Pat had put out her arms at the last second, or things would have been much worse. One side of her face was cut up pretty badly. She put a large snowball on top of the main cut and we helped her limp up to the house. That probably saved Pat from worse damage. She used the cold to reduce swelling and direct pressure to slow the bleeding. Ruddy repeated his "I am so sorry line" at least a dozen times on the way home. Pat said nothing until we approached the house.

She barked at Ruddy, saying, "Go home, you big oaf!" He liked my sister, but we never saw him at our house again. It looked terrible for a couple of weeks. We saw all the ugly colors: red, purple, blue, green, yellow, and finally back to pink. It was quite a day. I am sure my sister will never forget it. I don't remember her going sliding much after that day. But it sure didn't stop me and my brothers, Chris and Gary, from going out and down those steep hills. We even got crazier without her out there. We got hurt at times, but that's what kids do. Merry Christmas and may God's peace be with you and yours this holiday season.

Tomatoes and the Large Family Ways

The process of growing tomatoes started in March. In southern Michigan you can use longer season varieties down south, we used Rutgers. They have less water and more pulp which is good for canning. Marion's growing season is at least two to three weeks shorter. I have lived here for fifteen years, and I plant Early Girls and Better

Boys for the most part. We use to start some plants in the window sill to save time and money. We used organic or muck soil. We sowed the seeds in plastic cups and got an early start as a result. Plus, it was enjoyable to watch their progress. Our garden was huge over an acre about the size of a football field. We also sold canning tomatoes by the bushels. We grew about thirty bushels per year.

My mother sent us out to pick tomatoes that early fall Saturday morning. It was fairly early about 7:00 am; my sister, Pat, and my mom, Phyllis, were getting ready to can our tomatoes. Chris, my younger brother and I were the assigned pickers as our first task. I was about ten and he was four that fall it was nineteen -sixty. The day was windy and chilly with gray clouds streaming by with great haste. I could see that rainy weather was near us farm youth, we lived outside from March through October or more. You could already smell the swirling dust in the air.

Phyllis and Pat had the scalding water ready when we arrived with the first little, red, pull wagon load. Two bushels was all that could fit. We used half bushels to fill the wagon bushels as full bushels weigh over eighty pounds each. My sister and mom together unloaded the tomatoes unto the screened- in back porch. It was a nice place to sleep on hot summer nights. The skins come off in seconds after you drop them into the boiling water. I canned about thirty-nine quarts from the tomatoes in my garden this past fall. They seem to taste better than store bought ones. We couldn't pick all the fruits as no soft or green tomatoes were allowed. I, of course, had to sort out any bad choices my brother made as well. He was a little bugger at times like most brothers and would see if he could get me in trouble with mom. We also had to remove the stems as well. That seems simple but the thunder was rolling in, and the sprinkles followed. Trouble was in the air. We had clay soil, and that type gets sticky and difficult very quickly. My mom wanted at least eight bushels. I had to make some hard choices now. No way we could get that amount and still remove the stems out in the garden. I chanced it, and we raced the rain two more bushels delivered. We were now running as we picked. We were soaking wet with mud clinging to our shoes causing us to fall down in our haste. Bushels five and six delivered to the porch. We asked if we could stop - saying look at us but we were told only one more load, and you will be done. We knew the last load would be a difficult challenge. We hustled back to the muddy garden.

I suddenly slipped, thus crashing to the ground and that sent Chris down as well, as he was in the wagon. Rain pelted us, and it was difficult to see and walk. We started picking the last load; the easily found tomatoes, of course, were already in the house on their way into the canner.

Two hundred quarts was the goal. Most of the canned tomatoes were used to make Chili, Goulash, or as a direct vegetable side dish. The juice was drunk with breakfast for the most part. I seldom drank it because I liked orange juice but we seldom had that at our house. Some whole and some to be juiced. We were now doing our best, but we had less than one bushel. We had to chance it again and try to get enough without too many pink and rotten fruits. The mud was awful, and the wind and water were chilling us to the bone. Finally, we had nearly two bushels, but the gardens were empty of tomatoes. The trip up to the house took what seemed like forever. We made it up to the porch and heard, "what took you guys so long?". Those type of comments have always been hard on me. I have always done my best not to do that to others. I am however rather direct and blatantly honest, so I am sure I make mistakes in this regard. It is never my intention to hurt anyone.

You can, with God's help, turn a strict up bringing into a loving family of your own. I was blessed during my professional career to be at schools with the resources that allowed me as a teacher to give students wonderful opportunities to learn and grow. Plus, I helped raise a family that uses God's grace to help others. I pray a lot and continue my walk.

Fox Trapping in Days Gone By

My great uncle Glen was a very bright and interesting man. In the late fifties, you could get a legal bounty for a fox. The Conservation Department paid you five dollars in cash which was a silver certificate, for each dead fox. Plus, you could sell the pelt for about two dollars. That was a lot of money as minimum wage was a dollar and twenty-five cents per hour. So one fox was worth a half day of minimum wages pay in the 1960s - today that is nearly sixty dollars. It was not uncommon for my uncle to trap four or five foxes per day. He caught many other animals including skunks. You had to shoot them in the trap. I went with him whenever possible. He had a trap line of about one hundred and fifty sets as they were called. We drove around in a gas economy car, an AMC Hornet. It got great mileage for its times more than twenty miles per gallon. Farmers would readily allow us to put traps out, and Uncle Glen would tell them to keep their dogs and cats away if possible. Many people would let Rover out after a while, and we would catch him in one of the traps. A few people got mad but most admitted they forgot. If we got the dog a second time, we would pull the traps and find a new area. The traps were hold-strength so it seldom killed or maimed the dog. We checked the traps normally two or three times per week. People sometimes stole the fox and the trap. We never told people the number or locations of the sets. Plus, we stayed with people known to us over time.

The caught foxes were easy to disable and rendered dead. You pinned them using a forked stick and made a quick, strong step over the heart. That way no mark was left on the pelt. It was always interesting to go along to see what you would get besides foxes. I saw a wide variety of animals: mink, weasels, badgers, skunk, opossum, ground hogs, dogs, cats, squirrels, and of course foxes. We got one silver fox, it was worth fifty dollars, but this is the first time I ever told anyone.

My Great Uncle passed away over fifteen years ago. I still have several traps, but the bounty ended years ago. Maybe now we should have one on coyotes. The environmentalists would try to stop it in these times. I miss hunting snowshoe or varying hare. Trapping coyotes might bring them back to our area in time. Trapping was a fun sport, and you got lots of exercise doing it. It was a real challenge to try to out-fox a fox. They got away about half the time but being outdoors challenging nature what a thrill. Many of you probably could add to my story or make it more interesting. If you see me about, feel free to discuss your experiences. Peace be with you always.

Snowshoe Rabbit Hunting

Well, to set the record straight snowshoe rabbits are not rabbits at all. They are actually Varying Hare. They got the name because their coats vary in color with the seasons gray-brown to brown in summer, white in winter, and a mixture in between. Layman and local people in the Marion area call them snowshoes. This common name is the result of their large hind feet which allows them to dash about on top of the deep snow. It is rather like a human wearing snowshoes so you are able to walk on top of the snow without sinking in very far. If you have actually seen them on the run out in the wild, as I have, it's a sight to behold! I checked my facts in a reference book. They stated varying hare can reach speeds up to thirty miles per hour and can make leaps of ten to fifteen feet. Snowshoes are very handsome creatures in mid-winter. The ones I have seen or shot are nearly totally white. It's not uncommon to see them have their large ears tipped at the ends in colors of dusky brown leaning toward black.

Snowshoes are scarce around our area at this time to the best of my knowledge. All rabbit and hare populations rise and fall drastically. Cottontail rabbits' numbers seem to be a little more stable around here. That could be the direct result of some basic differences between rabbits and hares. Cottontails can dig burrows for themselves, but they often find and use underground dens dug by other animals - such as fox, woodchucks, badgers, or even skunks. Hares never hole up when chased, on the other hand when pressed cottontails will use any den anywhere. It was such fun to hunt in areas containing both snowshoes and cottontails. You could not be sure, in the good times, which animal might dart from cover. I had the privilege to be in a hunting party blessed with several great hunting dogs. Beagles seem to be the best dogs for hunting bunnies. Tall, long legged types chase the faster snowshoes and tires them out more quickly which is an advantage. The disadvantage is that slower cottontails hole up quickly when pressed by fast dogs. Slower dogs like basset hounds work great on cottontails because the rabbits might believe they can outrun these pudgy, long-eared dogs if necessary.

One time when I was out rabbit hunting many years ago, I started hunting near my brothers-in-law. They were much quicker on the trigger and better shots than me. So I decided it was best to get away from them so I might actually get to shoot my gun. At that point in my life, I had only hunted southern Michigan bunnies or cottontails. There are no varying hare near Kalamazoo. I had never even seen a real live snowshoe. I listened for the dogs and tried to guess which way they might go. That didn't work so well. I learned over time that rabbits and hares have great hearing. So even when being chased they apparently heard me moving about and never came my way. My father- in-law went away from us somewhere right from the start. I heard several gun shots during the afternoon. The snow was really deep, and I was about worn-out. All that trudging about without firing a single shot. I did see one cottontail and two snowshoes. Once I learned to stand still and wait quietly. I had not seen anyone for hours. Suddenly I smelled smoke so I followed my nose. That's when I found my father-in-law, Ralph McCrimmon, all warm and relaxed sitting on a stump, leaning over a lovely fire. He quietly smiled and said, "Find a seat by the fire and warm yourself." He asked me if I had shot at any rabbits. I sadly told him that I hadn't even fired my gun. That's when I saw his two large snowshoes. He was such a kind and pleasant man. It was snowing like crazy by now, but he was under an evergreen tree sheltered from the snow. The dogs had gone quiet. That meant it was time to go. It was a fun day just being outdoors and listening to the dogs at work was so relaxing. The very thought of our adventure makes me smile even now. Your soul seems to be recharged somehow whether you get any rabbits or not. My brother-in-law's each had several bunnies. I got a few rabbits on later hunts. But I doubt I could ever be as good a hunter as Grant or Gary, my two brothers-in-law. They each are able to successfully use their many years of experience to good advantage. We can't all be good at everything. Go out and find some rabbits, get some exercise, and have fun. God sure provided us a wonderful world to live in and enjoy.

Gift from the Indians

Early settlers, by numerous accounts, were taught the skills needed to make delicious maple syrup by indigenous, North American Indians. The sweet liquid or sap will soon be moving. The flow wells up from below as a weak watery fluid. You can get the best sap from Box Elder, Red Maple, and Hard or Sugar Maple. Sap can be collected from most trees, but it's not practical. The best place to gather sap is a sugar bush, a plantation of sugar maple trees where each spring the sugar-rich sap is collected. It takes forty to fifty gallons of sap to make one gallon of syrup. Sap is and was collected by pushing a hollow tube through the outside dead bark into the living layer or stem xylem. Forty gallons can be tapped out of a single tree in the spring season, which will soon be here. The maximum volume of sap can be collected when the nights are cold and the days are warm. This type of weather is needed to trigger the trees' natural process of changing starch into sugar. Maple trees and northern climates combine for these favorable conditions needed to produce the needed sugary solution. What tapping is actually doing is borrowing the water and minerals flowing to the organs of the trees.

Since I was a youth, I have been involved in collecting and evaporating sap to produce maple syrup. My grandfather on my mother's side, John W. Layton, had several sugar maple trees in his yard and in his small woods. I helped out by tapping, collecting, carrying, cooking, and eating the results of our efforts on some hotcakes. It took all day, but it is sure a wonderful memory. Several of my uncles and other relatives also made syrup, and my parents would loan me out to help do the various chores involved. Then I was a teenager I helped out at the Kalamazoo Nature Center. Each spring they collected a few hundred gallons of sap and on a given Saturday in early March; it was boiled down pioneer style over an open fire in a flat evaporator tray. The smells of the fire and sap boiling away the excess liquid create unique memories.

During my teaching days at the Career Technical Center in Cadillac, we tapped lots of different types of trees and compared the sap results. It was put in a two-hundred-gallon tank, and then we took it to a sugar shack. We ate the results on pancakes. It taught students how simple it is to do, the work required, and how to properly collect data when you are doing scientific projects.

A couple of years ago my wife, Gail, and I spent a lovely day at a modern sugar bush and newer style evaporator. Gordon DeHaan had a beautiful set- up over at Jack Eastway's place. Most of the sap was collected, piped, and pumped into a large collection tank. He had a gas fired evaporator and used a hydrometer to check the specific gravity of the sap. That is how you determine if it was ready to bottle as syrup. You can do things old school or use modern methods. But the smells and joy of being outdoors on a warm sunny day have the same living effect on me. I like ending the day with a product or result you can see, use, or enjoy. The gift from the Indians' maple syrup is another one of God's wonderful surprises. It is too big of a stretch for me to believe that it is a chance happening.

Volunteering in Belize

Many years ago in 1972 I helped develop 4-H clubs in the Central American country of Belize. It was trying and difficult work. The name of the country changed the same year that I lived there from British Honduras to Belize. It was a proud time for the new nation. The population is still small around 200,000. More than one-half of the people from the entire country are now believed to be living in the U.S. The vast majority speak the Queen's English, as well as Spanish. This makes them popular as employees for wealthy U.S. households. They often take jobs in the U.S. doing the work of maids, cooks, taxicab drivers, and the like. Most people living here like you and I can very easily understand them. They generally speak Creole among themselves. It is a mixture of English, French, Spanish, African, and a touch of Mayan. It is very odd to hear it at first, but you can quite easy begin to understand most of the talk after a few weeks of practice. The people I stayed with in Belize City operated a drug store. I stayed with their family, and they were very nice to me. I was stationed in Orange Walk Town; a district in Northern Belize for most of my fourteen months there.

Spanish and Mayan were used more often up my way as Mexico was a two-minute ride across the New River in many locations. The boats used there were actually called dories or dug-outs. They were made of trees cut in half lengthwise with a length of 10 to 13 feet. The natives would remove the excess wood with a small ax that looked more like a strong hoe - we would use in a garden. They were very tipsy to paddle and use.

Mostly I taught people, who were descendants of the Mayan culture more than a thousand years old, about vegetable gardening and livestock rearing. I am about 6'4" tall; by contrast, a Mayan woman is normally around 4'8" tall and man around 5" tall. They called me the "blond man," in Spanish. They made little reference to my height. Since I was a 4-H youth development program specialist, I spent most of my time focused on school children. I walked from remote village to village rather like, "Johnny Appleseed," only with a large supply of vegetable seeds from the Federated Garden Clubs of Michigan. I walked more than 12 miles per day on a regular basis. My visits started at the local school if school was in session. Each village had their own saints in this mostly Catholic area of the country so the children were not always around. Those days were sort of like kids here having Good Friday off. It certainly was disappointing to walk for two to three hours and see no one was around when you arrived. I eventually learned when to show up and give my demonstrations. The villages had no electricity, phones, running water or other taken for granted items of our world. It took time, but I gained favor where ever I went. My direct, honest style, I learned as State 4-H President of Michigan, served me well all those miles from home in a distant land. Values gained in the past can be transferred anywhere. God stood with me even when I did not deserve his grace. Some things can only be understood by faith, which I did not always have.

I faced many poisonous and deadly snakes, people thinking I had money thus wanting to rob or kill me, and dreadfully hot weather. The lessons learned and the grit developed there have followed me all the days of my life up to now. Working without pay or modern conveniences in a developing nation certainly challenges your spirit and will. The Holy Spirit must have been with me because I could have been harmed or worse countless times. The day before I volunteered to go I was offered a teaching job at Stockbridge Schools as well as a coaching position. Why I took the challenge even now, I am not sure. Life takes many twists and turns, and we are not always able to understand the meaning at the moment. If we are blessed with wisdom from above, sometimes we can later sort out the life journey's still before us. Can you take the road less traveled?

Time Warped

Suspension held to occur in the progress of time. Moving to Marion from the closest Michigan county to Chicago, Berrien County created that exact effect on me. Coming here from southern Michigan was most like being dropped off in 1962 and leaving me behind. Things are much different down there not better or worse just different. The I-94 corridor is a narrow strip of land, especially through foreign territory, which is densely populated including two or more cities. The key part of this definition to me is the foreign territory part. Those of you who have moved here from similar places can more likely identify with what I am talking about.

My story today will attempt to take you into a different world for a moment. It also might allow you to be thankful for the good things that you've got. The first major element is the traffic, being around big cities causes you to face the bustling traffic. Brisk and busy streets are the rule, not the exception. Marion got its first traffic light only a few years ago. The tension of navigating through this complex process can cause most people living at the slower pulse here great stress. For others use to the busier life, the rhythmic beat of the city makes them feel alive. It reminds them that the world is still vibrating along as it should be. Rushing here and there is like a grand competition for many. It begs the question for them, who can get there the quickest or fastest. When you hang with some city slickers, you'll soon discover that they will often argue over the fastest way to get from one place to the next. They both can be right that's the humorous part for me. Why because it all depends on the time of day, the construction projects that might have just started, or the ones that were recently completed, etc.

Second, has to be, what do you like to do for your life's work and with your down time. If you like fishing, hunting, cutting wood, viewing wildlife or going for a quiet walk you've surely got it here in Marion. Down in southwestern Michigan, you have college and professional sports, mall shopping, plays, orchestra music, movie theaters, and restaurants galore. So, if those type activities tickle your fancy, the big city life offers you a royal feast. The pace of life is simply faster down below. That offers those wanting a perceived more stimulating and busy lifestyle a chance to thrive in that type setting. My sister, Pat, and her family live right in the city of Richmond, VA. I live in the country side where there are no houses in several directions for more than a mile. She's been to my house and asks questions; like what do you do around here for fun? Her comments are usually something like, "this quiet country life would drive me crazy, there's nothing to do." That's the point. You have cleaner air to breath, time to read and reflect, and you don't have to rush around as often. I have enjoyed some elements of both my city life and my country life. Moving here has quieted my soul and calmed down my life. That is exactly why people come up north as they consider where to live during their retirement. No more traffic jams, the clear view of the stars in God's clear night sky, and even the northern light upon occasion. Can you beat that; it might prove difficult? Yes, for me it seems like time was turned back in 1992 when we moved here. Living up north seemed more like the days of my youth. People here are more likely to visit with their neighbors, drink coffee with friends, or even pray with fellow Christians for the benefit of others. How is it we are here, we're not always sure but, it seems pretty good to me.

What's Better than Fun?

The answer is more fun of course. People that know the best way to enjoy life realize artificial means are not necessary. Gambling, using illegal drugs, or drinking alcohol in excess, for example, are not in your best interest and certainly not mine. I am blessed to have no interest in these activities. Many young people who were my students over the thirty-two years in the classroom often could not honestly believe that I did not do or use these things. This is my story of victory in Jesus. I have no interest in controlling people that enjoy these activities at reasonable levels.

This holiday season our family rests, eats lots of candy, watches movies together, and plays lots of board games and cards. We have fun just being together and enjoying each other's company. It seems so simple, yet I hear so many sad stories of families and siblings fighting and arguing. I am not especially close to my brother or sister, so it is somewhat understandable. We had to work closely together so much on our farm that we didn't learn to have fun together. Probably because our family spent so much time working under the gun. When Christmas came around we needed a break from each other - that is my best guess.

My kids, two college graduates and a senior in college, went sliding the other day and had a great time. I went into my memory files to try to recreate many of the elements that I enjoyed as a kid. One is using a tractor, pulling a wagon around with bales of hay or straw to sit on for the ride out to the sliding hill with people you care about. I had gone to see a basketball game at MSU. My youngest son, Alex, drove the tractor and wagon since I wasn't there. It makes it all more fun when you ride out to the hill and don't have to trudge through the deep snow. Then you're worn out on the way back same deal. Another memory is a long toboggan with at least four people crunched together holding each other's legs. This is, of course, followed by a swift ride down when you can't steer very much, unless you're in front. It is common to find a few bumps or lumps on the way down as well. When you stop at the bottom you nearly always seem to have yourselves tangled into a knot. If no one is hurt, all riders commonly start laughing. You try to stand-up and someone loses their balance, and people pile up again. The day can't seem to end without some snowball throwing and a couple of face washes. Winter memories are usually good ones so get out there if you're able. I hope you have a great new year. Peace be with you and yours. Tell your family a couple of your lovely winter stories and enjoy the holiday season.

Spring Things

The weather will warm up sooner or later at least it always has in the past. I was walking on Saturday, and I discovered that even the angle and earthworms are mixed up this year. Thousands of them had crawled up onto the highway to get warm and out of the water. That wasn't working out so well for them, the cars were winning. The snow was flying like crazy. I had tried to wait it out. But after waiting four hours I decided to enjoy the beauty of the large flakes drifting down on me during my short rapid journey. There was no way to dodge them of course. Then I head up the driveway after my walk, several robins landed nearby. They were not seeking worms they were after soft bunches of grass. Female Robins lay four blue eggs each spring if Mother Nature is doing her usual fine work. The bird feeders were extremely busy during the heavy and brisk snow storm. Sometimes we may think wild birds are not too smart but somehow when food seems short and the weather cold, they rush the feeders.

The other spring signs are beginning the daffodils and tulips just popped up late this week. I took my tractor out for a ride in the woods. An Eastern Cottontail rabbit was out eating grass between snow squalls. He apparently was mighty hungry. I drove less than ten feet from him, and he barely glanced up as I passed by. A few geese and ducks were out paddling around in our pond. Only four days earlier some water fowl tried landing on the ice without much success. The recent rain cut through the remaining ice at long last. This late spring reminds us that we are not always in control of what can happen in our lives either. If you have faith in things from above, and you continue praying and doing God's will; we still are not sure of the timing of events yet to come. For many hope springs eternal and most of us are worn out by the long, difficult winter, we all just shared. You likely are ready for warmer weather and mushroom hunting if you're like me. With all the snow and rain it could be setting us up for lots of very large black, white and gray morels. May you have a summer blessed with tons of warm, happy moments with friends and family.

Kites, Rain, and Flowers in the Woods

Do we ever get tired of a warm breeze on a lovely spring day? It sure is refreshing and renewing to smell the air and feel the sun shining on your face. It seems especially true this year after the long, cold winter like we've just experienced around here. We each can recall the beloved saying, "April showers bring May flowers." Now our hope is that spring rains will soon green things up including those delicate flowers seen in our local forests and meadows. Strolling around the great outdoors can be an excellent way to calm yourself down. Walking at your pace, moving yourself about, breathing deeply, and simply relaxing, each move can help cleanse you both body and spirit. Sometimes it simply doesn't work out that way. But even then it gives you a break from computers, TV, music and cell phones all of which I strongly suggest you park out of reach.

Have you flown a kite lately? Spring breezes are generally stronger now than most times of the year. Tree leaves haven't slowed the winds yet. Modern Plastic Kites are generally easier to fly than older paper and wood styles. The newer ones are lighter with comparatively greater surface area. That means older folks like myself can have a spring fling with the wind. In other words, you might still be able to recreate the joy of kite flying. Locate a nice open field without power lines on a breezy day and put the kite into the sky. You remember slowly let out the string, as you run or briskly walk toward the wind and up it goes. New kites generally don't need a long, clumsy tail and nylon based string in thinner and stronger so run away kites are less likely. It is ever better to enjoy this activity with a friend or child. Smiles seem difficult to find in our rush-around world but being outdoors on a warm, windy day can turn your cares aside. Go grin and laugh at yourself trying to fly a kite, it doesn't cost much.

God intends us to enjoy the people and world we live in. But things are rather trying at this time in our land. For me, it helps to read a lot of books from the past, and I try not to watch all the negative news each day. Each of us hopes to figure out a plan for ourselves that refreshes and renews our soul. Kites and a walk in the rain might be an interesting first step in the right direction on that journey.

Lists, Mottos, and Goals for Life

Do you have a string of lists you use in your life? Personally, I have had them and used them for more than forty years. One of the oldest and most famous lists has to be the Ten Commandments of course. You can get all the lists you ever wanted to see by reviewing, "The Book of Lists." As a long time teacher I had a list of classroom rules: 1) Follow all instructions the first time given, 2) No talking while I am talking, 3) No touching other people or their things, 4) Treat people with care and respect, 5) Safety first to make your life last. Pretty basic stuff you've seen them for years but in my experience, they are not being enforced very well today in our American Schools. We are now rated either last or next to last in all subjects among the twenty-five most developed nations around the world. In the fifties and sixties when I was in school we were always in the top ten in the world in everything.

When I turned twenty-five years old, I wanted to get married, and I was having a difficult time locating the right kind of woman. So I developed a list that I thought might assist me in my quest. My use of it changed my life forever. This list has been shared with my children and others.

Several young men, I have met over the years have successfully used my list to find a wife. None up to now, at least to my knowledge, has reported any negative results. My Five Main Ingredients for a Successful Marriage are: 1) Marry someone whose maternal parents are still together and married to each other. 2) Marry someone who believes in God and is an active and professing Christian. 3) Marry someone who has an education and has their own successful career. 4) Marry someone that has their own hobbies, interests, healthy activities, but shares your mutually acceptable life goals. 5) Marry someone that is attractive to you on the outside and the inside. It took me three years to locate and marry a lovely woman that met all elements of my list, but thirty years later we are still together. My wife's and my parents were married for more than fifty years. The number one predictor of a long lasting marriage is whether the original parents are still married. This list of mine eliminates lots of people, but it was developed from experience and from doing what was best for me. Interestingly today's computer and/or TV ads tell you they use twenty-nine compatibility characteristics. E-Harmony and Match.com might be a consideration if you don't like Dale Johnson's List which is free but has no guarantees.

I mentioned in the title some other possible Ann Lander's type tidbits. My Life's Goal has not changed since nineteen sixty-eight, "Try to help other people as best I can to reach their best potentials." Next, my Life Motto, "Pray for a good harvest but keep on hoeing!" Last, my Life Verse, Philippians 4:6-7 "Do not be anxious about anything, but in everything, by prayer and petition, with thanksgiving, present your requests to God. And the Peace of God which transcends all understanding will guard your hearts and mind in Christ Jesus." We all have a certain amount of determination and spunk; it is up to each of us to use it to help our own life's journey. Its difficulty varies sometimes it's a long and winding road with a lot of steep hills to climb. Other times it's straight, flat, and easy to follow. I hope your present road is the latter and may God bless you.

Getting Ready for the Fair

April and May are when you should start your preparations for the local or county fair. You have to get the vegetables going and your animals fed and trained. If you wait any longer, you'll likely pay the price later. Cattle, whether beef or dairy, do better when you start sooner rather than later. As your animal grows and gets bigger and stronger the difficulty of getting them to go where you lead them increases. Hogs and sheep are the same deal, sooner is better than later. Horses are very challenging if you got a little slack during the winter. That's not good for you but time is growing short now, and it's time to rock and roll.

Step one is proper feeding and watering of course. Good clean water is the most critical element of care for all animals. Horses are the fussiest with water. You need to completely change it each and every day to keep them healthy. Healthy feeding requires all the things we need as humans. You probably know them, but here they are in review: Vitamins, minerals, fiber, protein, and energy, all in proper proportions. It is better to feed animals twice a day if practical. It is rather like you and I realizing we shouldn't skip breakfast. Three or four smaller meals is best for us humans and no late night meals. Regular feeding keeps your animals calm and healthy as well.

Step two is training your animal. There is no shortcut that I have ever heard of in preparing any fair animal for showing. You need to spend time with the animal. I feel a good way to start out is by washing your animal. If possible, use warm water since it's still a bit cool outside this year. Handling animals help them learn to trust you. Keep yourself and your temper under control because being loud, overly active and aggressive is dangerous. Animals can sense anger and the lack of patience with them. Although there are times when a firm hand is required with some animals. In general, rough treatment is not necessary or desirable for the most part. Quiet persistence is more likely to produce the desired results. I showed lots of kinds and types of animals over the years including showing for professional breeders. I have boxes of showmanship awards. That's nice but keeping your wits about you and being alert is extremely important. One moment of slack or overconfidence can get you trampled and/or severely injured. It might not happen at your home farm, but fair ready is another matter. Loud, sharp, and unexpected noises or big crowds of people can set-off an otherwise lovely and well-behaved animal. Plan to be with and around your animal daily leading, working out, brushing, grooming, talking, feeding, and simply touching your animal each help you and the animal get ready.

The final step is having confidence. You gain that in two ways: trials and experience. Some people are naturals with animals. Others try hard but they can't seem to get the knack of it. I had lots of practice over the years. We had upwards of two hundred and fifty head of dairy cattle, two hundred western ewes, fifty sows and bred gilts, ducks, geese, turkeys, chickens, a few horses, and Welch ponies. I have been kicked, rammed, bucked, bitten, trampled, and probably some others I can't remember. It taught me a very valuable lesson. Losing your temper after the fact does no good. I never lost my temper or yelled at one student at school in over thirty years. The experience gained from rearing animals can give you skills that will last a lifetime. God has plans for all of us. Discovering those plans is a challenging and difficult process for some of us. I have been blessed to see the plans and act upon them. Difficult times in the past can make you bitter or better, your choice. If possible, get your kids involved with the responsibilities of raising and training animals. They can go a long way in teaching your kids or yourself lessons for a lifetime.

The Wild Dog Pack

The weather was extremely hot and dry; it was late summer. Our herd of over one hundred head of mature beef cattle was out in the pasture. The temperature was over a hundred degrees Fahrenheit in the shade, with not a breeze to be found. The air was so still and quiet it looked like our farm was sitting in a cloud that day. All the spare money earned on our farm during the winter went to buy deacon calves. We had been taking all the bull calves from a large farm for years. Disaster loomed though we had no clue what was coming.

I heard a haunting sound from afar; multiple barking, growling, and yipping dogs. The noise, the disturbance, the trauma, the ugly memories, cannot be forgotten or pushed aside. The noise stopped, and the troubles began. A very hot day and heavy cattle being chased were too much. The result was twenty market-ready steers now lay dead, each torn apart by mad and blood thirty wild dogs.

In those days, a flood of city-slickers had rushed out to the country to live the good life and to get away from the rush around world. They thought at long last they could get that puppy. Then the puppies grew up and became troublesome. They thought, hey why not just let them loose, we're out in the country it can't hurt anything. Nothing can be further from the truth. But then a bunch of stray dogs becomes a pack of hungry, mean dogs. Wolves join together to hunt, and domestic dogs will do the same, back to their roots I guess.

The economic loss from the dead animals just about put us under. I was about twelve years old at the time. It sadly pushed me suddenly toward manhood without the fun of being a teenager. The struggle thrust upon us that day caused our family deep pain and suffering. That sudden loss lasted for years. When you have to live with pain you had no part of causing - that is a mighty bitter pill to swallow. Farm life forced me to become tougher and able to withstand most difficulties. Is that a good way to be brought up? I am not always so sure. Somehow I have been able, with God's help, to turn the tables. My wife and

I used love, Biblical wisdom, and responsibilities to raise our children. I believe it has worked well so far and only I hope I can still say that in the years to come. Wild dogs can cause big difficulties and my true stories today is a case in point.

One day you're happy and looking forward to a nice bike ride and swim with the neighborhood boys. The very next day you're a hired man hauling hay bales for the neighbors to help make the mortgage payment on your parents' farm. These stories make me sad at times. My hope in sharing them is to point out the stress and danger of living near a cliff of financial difficulties. Do your best to stay out of debt so that one or a couple of bad days won't throw you and your family into financial troubles. I pray none of you will have to face serious debt issues- it's not fun. Wild Dogs will likely always be a bad memory for me.

A Trip Down Memory Lane and the 21st Century

My wife joined me recently for a nice day-trip down memory lane. She suggested we go down to Cooper Center or Cooper, the area where I was born and raised about five miles north of Kalamazoo. My family, sadly in many ways, at least for me, have now sold the last of our three hundred acres of land and all three sesquicentennial farms. The area was named after the famous writer James Fenimore Cooper, author of "The Last of the Mohicans."

On my last birthday, my family gave me some money. I went to Walmart to look at digital cameras. Several young women were streaming in, and they were all gobbling up the same pink model. I questioned several of them as to why they were all choosing that exact one. They each happily slipped into some strange techno language-explaining all the lovely advantages and features, but the color still closely resembled lipstick. I swallowed my male pride and asked the male cashier for one of those pink cameras. He informed me that he just sold out, no more pink ones left. That was somewhat of a relief actually. Then in a flash, his face jumped to a look of pleasure. He informed me that he did have one gold colored display model. And if I was interested in that one he could take off an extra fifteen percent. The amount of the camera and the money I received was a match. The gold colored camera was a better match for me- a guy like me with silver hair. So I got the camera. I have since discovered some cool features of digital cameras: no wasted film and people at Meijer, Rite-Aid, Walmart, etc. will cheerfully help you learn to develop and crop the pictures. That's how you get the people in the pictures into the center of the photo and without all those wasted areas on the top and sides that you didn't want anyway. Also, you can easily brighten up pictures that are too dark, you can make prints about any size you please, and you can get three copies of one picture and ten of the next from the same data card. I've learned that now-days dragging yourself into the twenty-first century can be challenging and humiliating. I was at one point in time in my life pretty much on top of most everything in the world. Now, at least for myself, in one blink in time and I'm out of touch again. I know very little about "FaceBook" or "MySpace" for example.

Trips to your past often point you toward a cemetery, in my case to the Cooper Cemetery, where "my people" are buried. Many of mother's family are laid to rest there actually dozens of them. This is true since my relatives on my mother's side date back to the Revolutionary War and were in Michigan years well before it became a state in 1837. My sister, Patricia, once received a DAR or Daughters of the American Revolution Award. It was a necessary requirement that she prove to the selection committee that her family's ancestors had a direct connection all the way back to 1776. Like other people close to my age, nearly sixty, recording my family tree seems to interest me more than it did even a year ago. This became especially true for me after my brother, Gary, died suddenly and without warning at age sixty. Receiving "the call" informing you that your brother is dead is a very sobering reality. I used my new digital camera, which I mentioned earlier, to take photos of all the markers in my family's plot. It's a quick and easy way to record the proper spellings of all the names, birth dates and death dates. What's up with that dumb saying, "You can't teach an old dog new tricks," that's nonsense. So there are a few practical suggestions about getting and using a digital camera. Plus, they now cost less than half as much as they did only a couple of years ago. My final thought is that it was a marvelous day. Dozens of wonderful memories flowed back to me about my wonderful grandmother, Lida Caroline Layton. I loved her, and she loved me. My biggest hope and prayer for the future is that if I am ever blessed with grandchildren that I can be at least half as kind and caring towards them as she was to me. I used a portion of her name, for my lovely daughter, Amy Caroline Johnson who's presently teaching elementary school in Florida. Peace be with you all. Go get a digital camera, it's fun and easy to use. Don't be a chicken like I was for too long - you can easily learn to use one and people are loving my pictures! Remember you can fix most of your mistakes after the fact which is, "Way cool!"

Finding Your Voice and Other Things

Have you discovered the purpose and meaning in your life? That is, of course, the question for all times. The answer commonly changes throughout life. I have heard many people say they want to be rich. My definition of rich would be described as, "a life well lived for Jesus!" Others might think rich is having a large sum of money to spend on yourself along with your family and friends. When I attempt to write stories, my goal is to use my life as my voice. What you read and who I hope to be, are meant to be one in the same. I am beginning to understand that allowing others to see the humorous side of my life and being able to laugh at myself is increasingly important. Our present times seem difficult, and each of us can use a little laughter and a few grins.

On Saturday morning my wife and I were headed down to plant and water flowers at the cemetery. When we reached the end of the driveway, we got quite a surprise. Somehow a very large truck or bus had apparently run off the road and gotten stuck in our recently rain-soaked lawn. The ruts left behind were over a foot deep in places and over a hundred feet long. I whined and whimpered while knowing bad language wouldn't be allowed. The hassle and work that lay before me made me feel sick.

We then headed down M-115 and had gone less than a mile; when you guessed it - there was a young woman standing on the highway attempting to change her flat tire. My wife decided the "White Knight" should help so we did a quick U-turn. Gail would help by parking behind the young lass with the flashers on. It was a German car, a VW, so even the jack was one I had never seen before. There is no shoulder at all when you're headed southeast from our house. I had to almost lay on the pavement since the flat was on the driver's side front. The cars were streaming by at their normal crazy, fast speeds many more than seventy. The lug nuts had of course been put on by pneumatic hammer or torque wrench. I am rather heavy, and there I am using all my substantial weight to jump on the wrench handle. I only slipped off once. I finally broke the nuts loose after the third bounce. All the while I am thinking, there's no way an average sized woman could have gotten those nuts loose by herself. The tire was still extremely hot and was the likely cause of the blow-out. My bad - it was then I mistakenly noticed that all her tires including the spare were rather soft. So my wife again drafted me, the good old knight, to fill all her tires back at our house. All four tires were below thirty pounds of pressure. So of course, I'm left to get down and crawl around on the ground filling all the tires. I glance up and what do you know my wife and what turns out to be a young teacher from downstate, are now playing with her little kid. Gail loves small children, you guessed it, and the girls had just gotten the little boy out of his child seat. They were allowing the kid to pet our Collie dog, old Duke. Something didn't seem right about this whole situation or was it just me? The older, heavy guy does all the work - has to lay on M-115 to change a blown tire and is left to put air in all the tires. The ladies are laughing and playing with the little boy, Alec. Oh well, that's pretty much the story of my life. I do the work, and other people get the benefit!

We eventually got down to the cemetery to plant flowers and water. Once my wife gets to watering all those plants she has a hard time stopping. Dry plants draw in my wife like giant magnets. She'd already finished a dozen or so McCrimmon graves. But she can't stop there she always finds plenty of other dry plants. It doesn't seem to be such a bad hobby - I can live with it. Finding your voice in life is more about being the person God intends you to be. If you have the time to help someone in distress don't just pass by, remember the person you help could be your family someday.

The Bear Facts and Wild Animals

You just never know what you might see in the great outdoors. God's world is so beautiful and yet unpredictable. Last year I was out watching for White-tailed Deer during bow hunting season. When out of nowhere dashed a very large Black Bear. It was so rare and wild to my thoughts that I instantly started talking to myself. My brain said, "That was a bear; I just saw a huge bear gallop by!" The sighting was so totally foreign yet amazing even now I can scarcely believe it.

The very next day I was again out relaxing in my deer blind. The autumn leaves that sunny day were all aglow with the usual wonderful colors: scarlet, bronze, gold, and all shades in between. The air was clear and crisp with the added bonus of pleasant smells wafting about. Then a huge bird of prey crashed into our pond from high in the sky. The white-headed massive bird slowly rose with a small fish dangling from its hooked talons. You likely guessed it a Bald Eagle. The eagles rose high and then glided to a dead tree a not far away. It quickly disposed of the wimpy fish. The graceful and powerful bird lingered around our small pond and provided me with a special treat.

So a bear and eagle, two sights I have never seen before back to back, wow! My thoughts are wondering now what more can I expect. My eyes and mind are about worn out, and I doze off. I sense a sound never heard before stirring along the ground. I crept forward to gain a look see over the front edge of my box style, elevated blind. What to my wonder should appear, a waddling badger? Again a sight not seen before in my lifetime. Sure I have viewed badgers in zoos and on nature programs seen on TV but not in the wild at my house.

I often join several guys at ten o'clock coffee. My report of seeing bears was seemly taken with a grain of salt. But now my report is confirmed in a sad manner just this week. Sandy Merrifield spotted a dead animal near our house. It reportedly saddened her as she believed it to be our dog hit by a car. But on closer inspection, the dead animal was not our dog but was a bear. Yes, you read it correctly the first time- a bear! Gosh, this older guy was not full of beans or beer.

What a show and privilege seen just outside my door. Yes, retirement can be enjoyable and fun. Time to look about and enjoy the simple pleasures offered from above. As the cool people say now, "spot-on."

Class Reunions and How We Become Who We Are

Last weekend I went to my fortieth class reunion. Our class of 68 from Plainwell HS has had a reunion every five years since our graduation; this makes our eighth. Our class has always had a solid core of friendly and caring classmates. My discussions with various other people generally indicate this closeness is very uncommon. We had about 175 classmates, but only around fifty actually showed up. The class is now considering another uncommon activity. In two years most of us will be turning sixty so many of us are considering going on a group Caribbean Cruise so we can celebrate together. Last year my wife and I went on a cruise - I loved it. Gail enjoyed it as well. It was our way to enjoy something for us as we helped our children all get through MSU. The cost of the college expenses made it difficult to afford things for ourselves, and we're now saving for a December Wedding. That's life I guess?

Many of my classmates came up during the evening to thank me. I was a bit taken aback by these comments. They said they appreciated my friendly, polite ways. I was in the separate group of students scheduled to go to college. Some of the preps in my group didn't hang with or converse with the non-college bound folks. I always did - it was easy for me. I suffered often at the hands of my older brother. He picked on me a lot during my youth. This helped me realize reaching out and being nice was important. Dozens of times, when I was a child, I attempted to tell my parents of this ill treatment but always without results. Since my retirement, I have learned that this is rather common with older brothers. I had a younger brother, and I never picked on him. I realized even then that the sad feeling left behind after being messed with should never be passed on. This negative treatment helped me become more sensitive toward others. I have been able to use this to advantage over the years as a teacher, husband, and parent. Yes, bad treatment can be turned around for good. Somehow I was able to realize even at a young age that a bad situation could stop if you take responsibility to make it happen.

My class reunion was relaxing and fun overall. It has nice to see my friends, share a good meal, visit, and dance. Several guys in my class now have what I believe are called trophy wives or much younger new wife. Those old guys got worn-out rather quickly from dancing. The trophy wives wanted to dance more so I danced a lot with them. See bike riding, power walking, and cutting firewood in hot weather all added together can have an advantage - who knew? Only a joke, sorry - I went to the reunion alone so if I wanted to dance I had to find a spare or stay on the sidelines.

Following God's Will and the Deer Crash

Seeing God's plans for our actions can really challenge even the strongest believers. We may not be able to connect the dots at the time we are called upon to take a leap of faith. That was the case for me last week. The phone rang around seven am. I had been watching the Olympics late into the night for a couple weeks. The early morning phone call caught me unawares and cloudy in the head. The caller said his name was Byron and that he needed help. My first thought was, "So what, I am not sure I even know anyone by that name."

Probing my mind and stalling for a clearer explanation, I asked the man, what happened? He told me that he had just hit a deer on M-115 and that his windshield was blown out. The police had just arrived to take a report. I asked him if he was hurt and he said no. Then I asked him if anyone was with him and were they ok? He said yes and no he was ok as well. It was then that I, fortunately, remembered that he was from East Lansing, and his family attends the same church, University Reformed Church, as my three children. My daughter, Amy had babysat for the Lanes when she was at MSU. Bryon remembered when the wrecker driver told him the closest Auto Body Shop was Mike's in Marion and that Amy was from there. At that point, Byron called back down to his wife, Michelle, in East Lansing, an attorney. She got our number from the church directory thus the call for help from Byron. He was on his way to Traverse City to attend a conference when he hit the deer. Now the crazy part begins, I ask him where he was? He told me was not sure at first, then he spotted a road sign, Fiftieth Avenue and M-115. That location is right in front of our house. The deer he hit actually had run out from our land. He had called around and had discovered Cadillac was the closest place to get a rental car. I told him to hold tight, and I would come down to pick him and his passenger up in a couple minutes. I asked myself the WWJD question, what would Jesus do, while heading down the driveway and I knew exactly what to do. I picked up the guys, and we headed back up my driveway. I stopped the van, got out, and handed Byron the keys and told him to go ahead and head on up to his conference. He was somewhat in a state of disbelief. I told him that Amy loved being around his kids and lovely wife over her college years. She had mentioned more than once how nice the Lanes had been to her. My two sons had just moved to a house not far from the Lanes and that I would simply ride down the next day with my wife. That way Byron could simply drop off the van at the boys' house. We were bringing down some extra items the guys wanted anyway. That way no one would need to come get him at our house as he has three young children and I could simply drive our van back to my house. The thing is Byron has been wanting to tell his passenger about his faith and how God works in his life for some time. The right opportunity had alluded him. This entire situation provided Byron the right chance to give his testimony. The guy went on and on about how wonderful it was that someone that didn't know Bryon that well would help out like that. Byron shared some of this story when he dropped off the van. It was no big deal. I simply did my part and put the ball on the rim, and Byron slammed it down for Jesus. That's how things can go in the life of believers - can you honestly believe this situation was just an accident. I had no idea that my being helpful to a fellow Christian would lead another believer to share his faith and do God's will, but that's exactly what happened. Keep the faith and peace be with you all!

Fall and the Seasons of Life

Autumn is the season of life where I now find myself. It is a lovely place to be and hang out in. Fall is also my favorite season of the year: enjoying our beautiful leaves, breathing in the cool, crisp air, seeing and feeling a warming campfire, and having the time for reflection. These are the items that top my list. You may or may not realize - not all people of the world get the privilege of viewing the wildly colorful leaves each fall. You have to have the right outdoor temperatures and proper minerals in the soil. Iron is the element most responsible for the red color and the other shades involved. Sixteen major minerals are mostly responsible for plant growth which includes trees.

My roles are changing! The past saw me as a father of three children and teenagers, teacher of high school and college students, husband of a then younger wife, and church going Christian believer. My core values have not changed but times are changing me. Seeing why my grandmother acted as she did, mainly focusing on loving others, is becoming abundantly clear. You and I are challenged to keep our connections with our loved ones clean and connected. You have heard the saying, "With God all things are possible." This is a nice saying but without having the Holy Spirit helping you with your battle against Satan, it cannot be won.

I suffered a huge loss when I retired from teaching. I believed that a large part of who I am -was what I did. Part of me was lost for a time. Now I am beginning to understand what it takes to feel good and be the person God intends me to become. It is not a natural or easy process I can assure you. I have changed my TV viewing habits for example. Mostly I watch the Hallmark channel because it's full of wholesome values, morals, and ethics. I still cheer on MSU and look in on some sporting events. My time now leans toward reading Christian fiction and nonfiction books. I have read around two hundred books in the past four years. I find it a much better input for my life. I go to a men's prayer group, visit people in nursing homes, and spent time with people that need encouragement where they are in their lives. My teenage goal of, "Helping other people as best I can," is still my life's goal. I exercise regularly, eat a little smarter, and live for Jesus because that's all that matters for me. I pray you will find some encouragement from my heartfelt stories.

Have a great week and live a life that builds others up and you will become a bigger person.

Being Thankful in a Troubled World and Time

We need to always continue to love and appreciate the privilege of being an American citizen! There is a high price for freedom and not much appreciation for those who serve as soldiers, sailors, airmen, or marines. Today as part of a program at the Church we attend, the Lake City CRC, people volunteer to help families of active military personnel. Today a helper went to watch a couple of children so the wife of an active serviceman could go to work for a few hours. Simple acts of kindness and are a good way to show your love and support of our military families.

The twists and turns of life can be difficult to understand and straighten out in your mind. A clear example of that for me was a decision containing all those elements. The Vietnam War loomed large in my teen years and during my many years at MSU. I actually sort of won the lottery in some respects. The draft drawing was first held in nineteen hundred and sixty-nine, and I got a large number, two hundred and thirty-six. This larger number keep me in college and off the battlefield. My U.S. Congressman offered me an appointment to the Naval Academy in nineteen hundred and sixty-eight. It certainly was a nice honor. Had times been different I definitely would have taken advantage of a military appointment. The numbers of body bags being sent home during that war put a damper in my joining the military. The "what if," questions certainly still weighs on my mind. Going in person to actually see the huge, black marble Vietnam Memorial Wall in Washington D.C., with all the thousands of names of the deceased listed, sent a chill into me that I will never forget. I actually knew some of the individuals listed there. That is a stark reality. My knowing a high draft lottery number may very well may have kept me alive and still weakens me in the knees. Having served the public interest most of my career as a teacher helps me have some peace. I actually had better-paying jobs in the private sector as a salesman and a banker but returned to serving the public schools as a teacher. This fact gives me some comfort. We all should believe the opportunities for success in the USA are still favorable despite our current economic and political worries. God has a plan for my life and yours. Having faith and accepting Jesus Christ as your Lord and Savior offers you the free gift of salvation. We are blessed to live in the greatest country on earth. Sure things look a bit difficult right now but God willing our country will regain its footing and become strong again.

Retirement Watches

One of my distant cousins was a retired farmer. He proudly carried, for his timepiece, a nice pocket watch on a chain. His uncle had received it when he retired and passed it along to his nephew my much older cousin, Whitford Harrington. Like his unusual name Whit was a bit different in some regards. Personally, I have had the opportunity to meet thousands of people in my lifetime. Yet, he's the only Whitford I have ever come across. Whit was never married, and he owned a farm with fruits and livestock as his leading interest. Most of his life was spent near Alamo, Michigan. He asked me when I was a child if

I would like to see his pocket watch. What kid wouldn't want to see a cool watch that had a secret compartment on the back? Not many of my Swedish or German relatives ever displayed their warm fuzzy sides around children. They lived by the old adage, "Children should be seen but not heard." When glancing towards you, they seldom actually looked you in the eyes. If you tried to hang around the older folks - you would be called upon to get them all their drinks or snacks. You quickly learned that it is best to get lost if you didn't like being a very busy servant. Whit was different from the others. He showed an interest in me. He was a classic "English Gentleman"; proper but still he had a comical side. A good example of this was one Christmas my brother, Gary, got a plastic Detroit Lions football helmet. My dad jumped into the present opening conversation saying, "When I played football men wore real helmets made of leather." He jumped up and quickly produced his old green and gold one from his days at Coloma HS. This old helmet, of course, had no face mask like the one my brother had just received. This lead to the often repeated story by my dad about how he ran back a punt for a touchdown etc. We luckily were saved by the call to eat our usual Christmas feast. Whitford did not get up right away to join us. So my grandma, Lida, gave him a shout-out saying, "Where are you Whit? It's time to eat." We were all anxiously waiting to partake of the full blown turkey dinner laid before us. Whitford, a man of at least 80 at the time, slowly and quietly ambled into the dining room wearing my dad's old leather helmet. We all nearly split a gut laughing. That made for such a fun meal and day of warm memories. He looked totally silly and whacky wearing that helmet at the dinner table. My mom asked that he remove it, as of course, being that it's not proper to wear a hat in the house.

Whitford died a few short years after that happy day. He always treated me special. You know what - he taught me a great Christian lesson without even trying. The lesson here is simple. Always remember to take the time to be caring and kind to others, especially children. Whitford had a will, and I was in it. He left me the beautiful pocket watch I had always admired. I was only eleven at the time so my grandparents held it for many years. I believe my grandfather, John Layton, felt he should have received the watch so I didn't get it away from him until I was twenty-three years old. It is a lovely watch, and it still invokes enjoyable feelings.

Now for a brief bit about the second watch, I received four years ago. It was my last day of school at the Career Technical Center in Cadillac. The annual year-end picnic is always held that day. I had not planned on attending for fear I might become emotional. This was because after more than thirty years of teaching this was my last day. Matt, my friend there, came up to the new Agriculture and Natural Resources facility to get me and take me down to the main building. He explained that I needed to come down to the picnic. Because the staff and administration had donated money for a retirement gift for me and I should be there to receive it. So I rode down with him in his Jeep. First I was given a card signed by most of the staff and administrators, and there were several hundred dollars of cash included. I was very touched by the lovely kindness shown me. Relieved, I believed the luncheon had ended, but that was not the end of it. Then the Principal called me back up. He handed me a small package I quickly sat down believing the end finally had come. The people attending clamored for me to open what seemed to be a small box. I stood up and unwrapped the paper and peered inside seeing what turned out to be a jewelry box. The contents, a gold wrist watch, which was engraved on the back side. The staff enthusiastically clapped when they saw my great delight in its receipt. None of the other ten retirees received such a fine and thoughtful gift. That fact alone still touches my heart. God is good and the wonderful send-off I received that day will not soon fade from my mind - as it is now a wonderful treasured memory.

The Root Cellars and Fall Stuff

Digging root crops and storing them is difficult and dirty work. The good news in there is a sense of satisfaction in storing fall vegetables. You will feel a sense of pride and accomplishment. My family always raised a very large garden.

This story and the difficult days in the financial world last week get you to wondering. Will this pressure send us back to former times? Is it God's way of getting us back to basics? My grandmother, Lida, stayed at our house for years. Will these tight money times push families back together into one house, with a big old vegetable garden, and lots of canning and freezing being done out of necessity? It certainly is a cheaper living arrangement. In our case, grandma was not any problem. Lida was what people used to call, "An easy keeper!" If you needed someone to peel potatoes or carrots she was a ready and cheerful volunteer. Her eyesight eventually declined, and that irritated her. Why - because she loved to play cards and be around the action. She had a great sense of humor and could even laugh at herself and her age related shortcomings. Her most often used quotes were out of frustration, "It's hell to get old." And her more commonly used, "It's always later than you think!" We can't be so sure of what is down the road since the money world seems to hold lots of crooks with weak morals. Is a garden in your spring time future?

I still do have a vegetable garden not real big, but I have had one all my adult life. The variety in the old days at the family garden included winter squash of many types: Hubbard, Butternut, Buttercup, and Acorn. Lots of root crops like carrots, beets, turnips, potatoes, and onions. Each fall the digging began. Our main tools were spading forks, wooden potato crates, the little red wagon, and of course human hands. We had an unwritten agreement with a couple of the neighbors and relatives. Experience taught us that we, for our part, were good at tomatoes, bell peppers, squash, and beets. We did not have apples, and our heavy clay soil was not so good for potatoes. When the various crops were ready, the phone rang or the potatoes showed up. Sometimes we would have to go get the apples, or we would help pick up apples so our share of the cider could be pressed. We froze, canned, and stored in various ways all sorts of things. The amount of work required to put up enough food for the entire winter is huge. If you never experienced this process, it is difficult to believe. You worked every weekend and nearly every day after school. The mess you create freezing bushels of squash is close to crazy. You have to bake them, scrape them out, mix-up the cooked insides, stuff it into the plastic bags, label the boxes the bags go into, wipe them off, dry them off and arrange them in the freezer. Plus, you likely also had to defrost the freezer. Things we froze were: cherries, squash, green beans, sweet corn, strawberries, raspberries, applesauce, and lots of others crops. The canning namely involved: pickles, pickle relish, tomatoes, corn relish, green beans, raspberries, peaches, pears, beets, and corn. None of this work just happened. The crops controlled your life when fall arrived. If it got too hot or too cold, you had to scramble. Tomatoes don't like frost, so if clear and cool nights are near you, fire up the canner. If it gets, too warm potatoes have to be dug up quickly and put down into the roots seller. So growing and preserving our fruits and vegetables is a healthy way to get back to basics. Start now locating a catalog, then locating a sunny site, and start planning. You might start small and see how it goes the first year. Get out there have fun, involve the kids, and teach them to appreciate the benefits of hard work and fresh crops. Getting down in the dirt isn't so bad, you might even learn to like it.

Should've

Do not get caught with a life still full of "should haves." A life containing regrets and missed opportunities will haunt your soul. Recently a good friend of mine suffered a huge loss. His twenty-month granddaughter quickly died of a rare cancer. I drove down to the Pontiac area for the funeral. David, my longtime friend, gave a stirring and heartfelt eulogy. It was full of healing thoughts and wisdom. He had visited me up here during the summer. We had a fun and enjoyable couple of days of scooter riding and catching up on each other's lives. It is sometimes too common for me to use my spiritual gift of discernment. Having such an ability allows me to come to know or recognize things beyond the norm, and that can be a troubling and unwelcome burden at times. I strongly suggested to David, even prior to the visit, that he should consider spending more time with his granddaughter and daughter. He listened and responded beyond my wildest dreams by selling his prized motorcycle and purchasing a high mileage car. He then used the new car to frequently commute back and forth to see "his girls" as he called them. The car allowed him to take the girls to special places and share what is best known as, "Quality time!" You see he identified a priority and acted to keep it from turning it into a, "Should've." We all face lots trials and difficult decisions in life. But the most important thing is how we respond when they come our way.

My dad, for example, failed to tell me he loved me until he was about ready to die at age eighty-six of prostate cancer. And he only told me then because my mother prompted him to say it. He either didn't know or didn't understand how nice it would have been to hear those simple three words. The same holds true for hugs. I don't ever remember him hugging me or seeing him hug anyone else. Hardened old timers were sometimes taught that showing your emotions was a sign of weakness. I hug my sons and daughter nearly every time I see them. It's part of how my wife and I live our lives. I also tell all my children I love them continuously.

You see I try hard to avoid the world of should've. Doing things you need to do and avoiding difficult choices won't always help. When you have the opportunity to do what is best, even when it is more difficult, it takes the road less traveled. Is God presently sending our nation a warning that we need revival and repentance? Or maybe it's just the greedy people on Wall Street and uncaring bankers putting thousands of people into loans they couldn't afford just to earn commissions. Our present economic times are causing us much distress and things seem bleak. I suggest you try your best to avoid all the, "what ifs and should've," that you can in your life.

Thanksgiving is for Each Us

This year challenges our spirits more than most recent years. The lack of jobs and in turn hopelessness are haunting our area, state, nation, and world. Being thankful for the good things that you've got are for many only a dream. A warm home, loving family, and a shared meal may be things once taken for granted. But this year these basic things may have grown in favor. One of my three children is scheduled to spend the holiday meal with my wife and me. We are looking forward it. We play board games, read, relax, and enjoy each other and the time to spend together. Sure it's the simple stuff, but I appreciate it more each year I live.

My dad and brother both died in the past couple of years, and each loved the turkey dinner, football, and the day off. Reflecting back can be somewhat troubling for me since my brother died suddenly and without warning. It makes you wonder. What should you be thankful for? I am not afraid of death, but dying doesn't seem so fun.

Is your life all about you and your desires or is it about others and their needs? A life lived in a broader realm can make you stronger and wiser. A self-centered focus will limit who you are and are likely to become. I have more time in retirement to help others beyond the norm. I realize it is a privilege. Sure I did not have the toys of my times like snow machines, jet skis, or quad-runners. Now I don't have to pay off the bills for those items.

Did I miss out on a lot of fun or did I do better not having to pay for them?

Enjoy the day and be engaged with your life. Bring as many people into your circle of love and friendship as you can. You'll live longer and be more fulfilled if you do. Happy Thanksgiving!

Dorothy Goes Home

As luck would have it for nearly fifty years, the town of Marion has had two Dorothy Robinsons. Two brothers, Merlin and Norman Robinson, each married ladies named Dorothy. So as to distinguish who you were speaking of it became customary to refer to each through the use of a code name. City Dorothy Robinson meaning Dorothy Ann who lived in town and for Dorothy Robinson not living in town she became known as Country Dorothy. This cleared up who you were speaking of. Most people in Marion knew City Dorothy as the Marion Schools Elementary Librarian.

I did not go to Marion Schools although our three children did. My wife's family, the McCrimmons, are related to the Robinsons. I mention this because it is how I came to know City Dorothy. My sister-in-law who lives in Florida was not able to see her father very often as he lived at Autumn Wood Nursing Home in McBain. So as to be of assistance I started visiting her dad, formally of Cadillac. In time he was not able to talk with me and would fall asleep during our one-sided conversations. He died shortly after this development. His roommate Merlin seemed to need some company. So each Thursday morning after my men's prayer group that meets at 7 am I normally stop by to visit Merlin at Autumn Wood around 9 am.

City Dorothy fell and was injured at home. This made it necessary for her to come over to Autumn Wood for care and therapy. She came to know that I visited Merlin so it became common practice for her to wheel down to Merlin's room to join in on the weekly visits. Dorothy shared with me her plans and struggles. She was determined to do her therapy so she could return to her beloved home in Marion. She also kindly encouraged me to continue writing my Marion Press stories she reportedly enjoyed. For many weeks I got her report of how long she was able to stand up alone. She worked hard to reach the time standard requirement necessary to for her to be able to go back home again. Dorothy also faced the side effects of her other treatments. Through all the trials and difficulties she faced not once did I hear her whine or complain. We go visit others during difficult times in hopes we might somehow be a small blessing to them. Seeing Dorothy's grace and determination during difficult times was a blessing to me. Why, because I learned a life's lesson - do your best in all things and don't complain. I pray if I face this situation I can be half as strong in spirit and faith as her. She wanted so badly to make it home, and I believe with all my heart that she did make it home and now rests with the Lord. Peace, our prayers, and comfort go out to her family and friends.

Proud Father Welcomes new Daughter-In-Law

Alex McCrimmon Johnson married Conchetta (Higgins) on December 13th to become part of our family. It has been a wonder day and year for Alex. He and his now wife, Chetta, each graduated in four years from MSU with honors and both are now graduate students there as well. Many people asked me questions about the future bride. Mostly they ask if you like her. That is a loaded question and one that you dare not answer, especially if the answer were no. However, in my case, I told Chetta that she was irritating because I couldn't think of anything I didn't like about her back when they were first engaged. Her response was totally disarming saying, "You just don't know me well enough yet!" I haven't changed my mind about my now daughter-in-law.

The very lovely wedding was held at the University Reformed Church in East Lansing where the bride and groom are each members. Several people from Marion made the truck down to support the couple and luckily the winter weather was agreeable. Alex's brother, Eric, was the best man and his sister, Amy, was a bridesmaid. It was a picture every parent dreams might happen. Alex and Eric stayed together for the past few months because they are very dear friends as well as brothers. They roomed together in the dorm at MSU a few years back not to save money, because it didn't, but because they enjoy being together. Amy likes Chetta a lot and loves the idea of now having a sister that she didn't have as a child.

Chetta is student teaching this semester and MSU which has a very strict set of guidelines about missing days at school. Alex as well works at MSU as a teaching assistant so their honeymoon was a day at a Lansing area bed and breakfast. They paid cash and will start without any wedding debt, and that is a great way to start things out for a newly married couple especially in these uncertain economic times. Congratulations to Alex and Chetta

Johnson and may God's peace be with you now and forever.

The Layton Rocking Chair

My Great Grandma, "Jo", Josephine died in 1960 when I was ten years old. She loved her rocking chair – claiming it was her place to "mull things over." I still remember helping her out of the chair as she was in very poor health. My Grandpa got the rocker because the caning was shot and broken as Grandma Jo stayed with Orlo and Marie Norton, John Williams Layton, my grandpa's brother in law and his sister. Phyllis Marie, my mother, wanted my grandfather to get rid of the worthless, old broken rocker. Jack, as they called him, was a very bright and clever man. He never had the chance to live out his life-long dream to become a doctor. It cost over $50 at that time to have the chair recanted and $40 to have it refinished. He did not have the money to have it fixed, so he declared it was his mother's beloved chair, and he would do the fixing himself.

Jack slowly and painfully cleaned off the old finish and worked quietly on it down in the cellar so no one would know what he was up to. I used to ride my bicycle over to his house five miles, so I could talk with him and watch the chair come back to life. Jack taught me to take the time to "fix what you can and make things last by doing things right." The chair was now clean and refinished with all its caning stripped away. I asked Jack if he knew how to fix the caning and he said no, but he had found someone to teach him at a training school near Plainwell, a state-run facility. He went up there several times to learn how to cane. Plastic was new to the canning world so Jack opted to use it as it was supposed to last longer. It took him all winter to redo the webbing but when it was done it was better than a new chair and looked great. My mom, Phyllis, tried to take the chair away from her mother, Lida Caroline Layton, now that it was nice, but my grandmother refused, telling my mother as long as she had breath she was keeping it. And if anyone was going to have it Dale gets it. After all, he helped Jack fix it! Lida reminded Phyllis that she wanted to throw it away, but now that it looked good she wanted it. So in truth, it was never Phyllis' chair. It was really always my rocker. My grandpa and I brought it back to life, and I have now given in to my daughter, Amy Caroline. I pray she will feel the love and magic of the old rocker, try it out with new light on the real story of Lida Caroline and the magic rocker.

The Teacher's Request for His Students

Your time meter's rolling the days passing by,

All I can ask is that "can you but try."

Life can be tough that's no lie,

Do your best and never say die.

Be a bit friendly try to say "hi,"

Keep the questions coming always asking "why".

Always moving up toward the sky,

learning by doing is our battle cry.

A good education can help you fly,

now have a great life, remember to try.

It won't be long and we all say goodbye,

Here's hoping you soar and make us teachers sigh.

The Wintery Day

I sat there rocking on this wintery day - glancing out my window watching hungry birds at play.

There was a storm a brewing not far away. Many types of birds to see - doves, cardinals, and a chickadee there were many beyond those three - nut hatchers, sparrows, and juncos now added to the list for me.

I had given the birds a fresh treat and watching them now on a comfortable seat.

The mass of sparrows so proud made a stand but with the blink of an eye they now disband - for a large woodpecker alone scares off the whole band.

He ate his fill and glanced all around - only small birds took to the ground.

Fresh birds approaching hit a new low - the big white flakes arriving had taken its toll.

The wind picked up in the darkening sky - it's the way of the wind we know not why.

Only God can answer, I shall not try - enjoying God's blessings as the days fly by.

All one day from the wintery sky.

Beaver Pond Evening

Did you ever see a beaver working in the wild?

Did you ever see a white-tailed deer playing like a child?

Have you seen a muskrat swimming in a baby brook?

Have you seen a timberdoodle fly by so fast you barely got a look?

And then I saw a cottontail bounce along in the grass so tall,

If that were not enough two mallard ducks sailed by and overlooked us all.

Christmastime Rhyme

Christmas is the time of year,

To think of families and friends far and near.

A cozy fireside dream time is here,

Those winter winds that chill the deer.

Now take a reflective moment to peer,

At yourself – your life in a mirror.

If what comes back makes you cheer,

Remember to give that to others you hold dear;

If what comes back makes you fear,

Remember faith and God this time of year.

The Hungry Pond

Deep wet snow covered the ice on the farm skating pond. At least that's the way us young farm boys saw it. A brisk north wind swirled the arctic air through the now leafless black willow trees. In summer they guarded the football-sized water with cool shadows. Today winter weather blew through without ceasing, and we saw above a gray sun lost sky.

A raw and rare day but it was the day after Christmas. So a special treat was at hand for some ambitious lads. The farm chores were done already and were now behind us in the day. A wild and fun game of broom hockey on ice was at hand. The enemy we six guys faced was sloppy wet snow, but scoop shovels in the eager young skilled hands that had each tossed thousands of bushels of ear corn and grain were no match today. Spirits remained high and hopeful. The cleared area grew with a speed: city slickers would find difficult to imagine. Because strong, young, and determined farm youth in the sixties were no couch potatoes, like youth of the nineties. A day of rest was nearly unheard of it. After all it could ruin our futures. Just ask our parents who sat inside a warm house eating

Christmas cookies and drinking hot beverages. There they speculated about a lazy new generation of kids. Broom hockey was to be played today with a real hockey puck that David, a neighborhood boy, got for a Christmas present the day earlier. A variety of house, farm, and corn brooms were the sticks to move the puck. Some guys used the dozer method, and some tried crafty, back-and-forth motions. No matter each style could score if you played long and hard enough. The goals were two mismatched grain buckets at either end. The snow was about gone. Tired, old, and often rusty skates were the best we had. Some players had to run with farm boots and no skates. The apparent preferred uniforms were patched bib overalls worn over your barn clothes. They offered some protection from the puck but had good flexibility without much reduction in speed. Coats were now tossed to the side. Leather gloves and stocking hats were necessary because broom whacks from our older brothers were coming especially when they got tired and we younger boys still were full of energy. Tripping calls were not part of this game. Neither was offsides or icing. They were called break-aways and used for resting when you got tired. The ice was good today but it was very thin in the southwest corner portion above an obvious underwater spring. I was a slightly younger player and volunteered to fetch the puck from the thin tan ice over in the bad ice corner. That policy worked well because my team got extra possessions and a resulting a lead of 4-2. My big brother hated to lose especially to his little brother and all the other little brothers a seemly outmanned team. That's when the excitement began. Gary, my older and heavy brother, went to get the puck on the thin ice above the active spring. You can guess the rest. Sure enough he fell through and he sank in a rush. The area was not real deep. But up to your chest in water on a fifteen-degree winter day is not a good thing. He was mad and soaked. We got him out by giving him a broom as a towrope. He was cold his sweatshirt and pants all began to freeze instantly. Gary was smart enough to head immediately up to our house but after a few minutes the soaked clothes turned stiff as the tin man in the Wizard of Oz. God it was funny, but we didn't dare laugh. He couldn't walk at all by the time he reached the barn. So we laid him on a four-man toboggan and dragged him toward home. My mom was glaring out the window wondering what we were doing. She had warned us not to go near the spring. She blurted out a hostile "I told you so!" speech before any of us could talk. Although she quickly saw my brother was hurting and about frozen stiff. We really didn't know what to do at that point. My mom and we kids had to thaw him out without making a wet mess in the house. His snaps and zippers were solid ice and he was shivering. His teeth chattered and he was blue with cold. Our past laughter was replaced by worried looks, which had replaced the joy of the hockey game. Mother directed me to run down and shovel some coal into the old octopus-style furnace. I dashed below into our Michigan cellar, a dirt-walled basement. I stoked up the old girl and opened up the flue as wide as it would go. The orange amber coals inside burst instantly into blue crackling flames. We then placed Geggy, Gary, upright on top of the warm heat register. Gary was still frozen like an icicle. Luckily for him he was starting to drip but still could not bend. He was now leaned up against the wall still stiff as a board. Paul Early, the neighbor boy and I, Dale the younger brother, kept him upright. The water was now dripped off him like a spring thaw. Gary's face was starting to change from blue- gray to white; that was the good news. The bad news - his teeth still rattled like a grandma chopping nuts on a wooden board. The water drizzled off him in a steady stream. His chattering started to slow and his skin color moved from that ashen gray to dull pink. He could now move his arms and legs. The ice was nearly gone. The final chunks of ice dropped down through the register with a hissing sound and a steamy stink filled the air. My mom had started filling the bathtub with warm water. The thawing out of my brother was progressing favorably. Gary was normally somewhat brash and confident but the cat apparently got his tongue this day. Mom got him into the bathroom. He slowly tracked in still he shook and could scarcely mumble. His soaking wet and icy clothes were peeled off. Gary stumbled into the tub and slumped into the warm water. He was a tough strong lad but the combination of the chill of his formally near frozen state and the warm water was nearly too much. He moaned like a wounded bull when he was fully submerged. His language was not what a mother can tolerate. Even the strong-willed Phyllis, our mother, said nothing. We all smiled broadly at each other especially since she could not see us and because his outburst told us the worst was over. Mom told us to heat some water on the stove. We were now sweating up a storm and we were panicking because the snow and ice had puddled everywhere that we had stood.

Phyllis attended to Gary in the bathroom. We were all going to get a whopping if we didn't get the water soaked up with due speed. I scrambled to strip off my snow gear and then I dashed to the cellar to get some clean rags. Gary was still not warmed up at this point. My sister Pat now entered. She had just returned from babysitting at a neighbor's house. This was very good news because she could more safely carry the hot water without spilling it. Plus mom liked her. She was the oldest and only daughter. Pat, I explained with a hushed cry, could you please stall mom. We'll really get it if we can't clean up the soaked floors before she comes out of the bathroom. Pat was not sure what was going on so I told her that Gary had dropped through the ice. He had gotten nearly froze stiff on the way up to the house. He was now in the tub warming up. Pat was a good sister and she understood the trouble we were in. She further knew that Phyllis with a blown fuse was not a good site for anyone. Pat was a quick thinker. She took charge without missing a beat. Hot tea was a calming potion on Mom. So the real life drama play was on. Not only did Pat bring in the hot kettle for Mom but also she took hot tea and strawberry tarts for Gary and her. The steam was slowing now from out of Phyllis' head figuratively. Pat's ploy was successful. We had the floors dried, dishes done, and wet snow clothes hanging in the basement drying peacefully. The neighbor boys scatted and were down the road with speed. They knew from experience that it was best to be on their way at such times. Brother Chris and I slid off to bed even though the hour was early (it was barely dark out). Pat told us go and she would tell mom we were cold and tired. We each found a comforting book and began listening for mom. We always had our plan if anyone came up the stairs where we always slept. Our light would be turned off. We would act like logs in the forest. The polite scam was a winner; no one tread up the stairs but a still cold Gary. He quietly slipped into bed and was asleep as fast as can be. The tale ends with no serious damage. Our teamwork and quick thinking was great damage control. Thanks to our kind sister, a fast clean-up and a quiet and early bedtime. Plus, Gary didn't even get punished, except for the cold dip. One he will probably always remember - his winter swim in the pond.

Ice Fishing - The Hole Hopping Method

If you enjoy ice fishing like I do today, I will share a style that will definitely increase the number of fish you will catch. This is a more active and aggressive method. Basically, you work a little harder and cover more areas of the lake. First, you should drill and skim the ice out of at least ten holes before you even think about starting to fish. If you cover those holes and have no luck repeat the process with an additional ten holes. Drill the holes about twelve to fifteen feet apart in a straight line from shallow toward the deeper water. I like to start in about ten feet and try to reach fourteen feet or so. If you hand drill use a six-inch laser auger; it is the fastest and takes less effort to cut through the ice than an eight or ten-inch size. This item costs about forty dollars. When the ice gets thicker, say beyond ten inches or so I like my Jiffy Stealth eight-inch power auger the cost is around $400 dollars. It cuts very fast as it is a professional model that self-centers when you start each new hole. It weighs less than all other standard models, and it is a two horsepower model. Second, buy or customize yourself a four to the five-foot ultra-light rod. This is accomplished by hot gluing a spring bobber directly onto the pole. Be sure the spring reaches about one inch beyond the end of the rod tip. You can buy a Cadillac Brand ice rod; it's four-foot-long, and this pole is specifically designed for this purpose. They cost about twenty-five dollars these poles are so light in action that no spring bobber is necessary which makes getting started easier. My choice is to add a small open face reel - these cost about fifteen dollars. A reel allows you get the fish out of the water more quickly and back fishing sooner. I use high visibility two-pound gold line. It is easier to see your line if you break off or want to change tear drops on sunny days. I've seen people using many other line colors: green, clear, black, blue, and the latest new color red line. Third, tie on a tear drop. My choice is size # ten glow type, Moon Jigs with gold speckles are my favorite. This jig is made in Hastings, MI by K & E Tackle on the web at www.stopperlures.com. I get them at Pilgrim Village in Cadillac west. You can use other tears drops like Marmooska Jigs, or Swedish Pimples size 2 ZB. The color I would start with is bright green, followed closely by purple, or orange. If you fish past dark use glow lures, they're best as they can be charged up -causing it to glow or give off light. An HT light costing about five dollars makes it visible in the dark under the ice for the fish. You simply shine the bright light on the tear drop to activate the lure. Fourth, use live bait. I use spikes which are very tough and will outlast wax worms, mousies, wigglers, or minnows. All of these listed will work of course. I purchase a large amount; one thousand at a time these last me all season, and it saves time and money. That amount costs fifteen dollars, but you have to be order ahead of time as I then don't need to go get bait again all winter. They come in a plastic container the size of a one pound soft spread butter. You'll need to keep them in the fridge. Last, put on your chosen jig find bottom with a small clip on weight. This is simple, to do, attached it to your tear drop and dropped to the bottom of the lake. Attach the line to the line stop on the side of your reel and crank it back up. Take off the spring weight add on the spikes through the eye end, the end with the two dots, and drop them back down. It's best to put on several spikes or at least completely cover the entire hook. I start about three to six inches off bottom and jig my way up to two or three feet off bottom. I slowly raise up the lure about three inches between jigs. I then jig my way back down to six inches and repeat that for at least three rounds. If you hook a fish make a mental note of how high up you were off bottom so you can get back to that exact depth quickly. It is common to get several fish in a short period if you hustle back to the proper depth. My choice is four, one to two inch quick tugs, then a five to ten second still period. The key for my method is if I don't have a strike within five minutes I crank up and move to a different hole. I stand up all the time and reach down toward the ice with my long pole. I find myself becoming lazy if I sit on a pail or in my portable shanty too long. If I do get cold and sit in my one-person portable shanty with the heater on. I then drill two holes a foot apart and switch to two thirty-inch diddling rods with the same setup. Sometimes I stack two tear drops one foot apart on each pole but your chance of becoming caught under the ice increases when pulling up the fish especially on the bottom lure. I fished six days last week and caught an average of twenty fish on each trip. I keep notes on the people I meet so I can hopefully remember their names. This is useful so you can gain information on what was working for other fisherman so you find the fish faster for yourself. Stand with your back to the wind I wear two hoods and lots of layers of clothes. The fish seem to taste better in winter so get out there and good luck. If you see me in town or on the ice, I will help get started if you have further questions. I do not use electronic fish finding gear myself although it can work and be helpful.

Our Florida Trip

Last week my family and I took a quick trip to Florida. MSU, where we all attended college, was playing in the Capitol One Bowl in Orlando, Florida. We got tickets and rolled south. We stayed in Lecanto with my daughter, Amy, who is a school teacher at Seven Rivers Christian School. It is a Presbyterian Church-sponsored school system. I'd say it is somewhat similar to North Michigan Christian School in McBain. Amy teaches third grade - it's her second year there. Since it was Christmas vacation, she was free to entertain us. We drove straight through; it took twenty hours. Leaving at four in the afternoon works out well for us as we have driven to Florida at least a dozen times. Things in life have a way of working out if you stay alert and are ready to respond.

Some of you probably are wondering why anyone would go to Florida and back in five days? Well, the planets were aligned for us to make the trip. We had several drivers, a mini-van with the seats removed in back and that makes into a nice bed. This allows for the next driver up to sleep until their turn at the wheel. Gas prices are low right now, we paid as low as $1.39/gallon. The extra bonus was the airline wanted $150 for my daughter to take her small dog one way. We avoided that expense by bringing it with us. It is a carry-on size dog, and it rides under the seat. That price is just plain crazy. We made it down with no delays, and the weather was great. We rested up and put a large puzzle together. One of our simple ways to have a family activity to share over the holidays.

We drove over to the game MSU vs. Georgia. We saw Sparty, the Michigan State University Mascot, outside the Stadium and had our picture taken with him. The temperature was nice and the sun shown off and on during the entire game. The MSU and Georgia bands both played and that was fun. A huge group of local cheerleading teams all dressed alike, numbering at least 400, also performed, and that was very impressive. We had fireworks and a jet squadron fly over so low it hurt your ears a bit, and you could feel the wind from the F-118's as they passed over the stadium. State lost after leading at halftime, but it was a wonder trip and adventure. If you have the chance to go see a bowl game you might enjoy the event and in the process create a family memory.

Reflection Season

The days are real short now, as December 21 was the shortest day of the year, in terms of the day light hours. I was home today enjoying the quiet and watching the birds eat their fill after the big snow storm. I was tired of music, TV, and noise. I was peacefully resting looking at our Christmas tree; it's my favorite kind, a white spruce. This year's tree is especially rewarding as my children had planted it fifteen years ago when we first arrived here to live. None of them have seen it, but I am willing to bet they'll be pleased. Today I am reading 'Unafraid' by Francine Rivers. It's the story of Mary, mother of Jesus. No matter how hard I try, I still can't quite put myself is her place or even in Joseph's for that matter. Faith and grace are so simple, yet so difficult to fully comprehend.

Today I am dog sitting for a Florida dog of my daughter's. It's called a Pom-Chi. The short little guy went to the door to go the bathroom, and the snow was over his back in depth. I wondered what would happen when I let him out and to my surprise, he charged right into it with great delight. It made me laugh and lifted my spirits. The crazy little fellow ran around in the deep snow as if he had a case of cabin fever. Which I guess he did as I had kenneled him for a few hours while I went ice fishing. The fish were biting some yesterday, but today only the small ones bit.

This global warming is getting a little tiring, isn't it? Moving the snow in and around in my yard is not so bad, but having multiple lanes of snow continually piled up at the end of my driveway would get on any person's nerves. Six times plowing it in a single day like today is annoying. However, the upside of living on M-115 is if you really need to go someplace the road is usually open.

All our children will be home over Christmas for a few days. We'll celebrate Jesus's birthday, go to a local church for a Christmas Eve service, open some gifts, eat lots of good food, appreciate our many blessings and laugh while playing cards or games. How do you celebrate Christmas? I hope you can share it with family and friends. What more could you ask for?

A White Bird in the Flock

The black birds are gathering for their annual trip south. You who live in the world I have lived in know this is normal for fall. It is not possible for an old farm boy like me to believe Darwin. He is "whack" as the young people would say on the net. Does one turtle or one eagle look one bit different than it did a thousand of years ago? All things were made from above as far as I can see, from the stars in the night sky to air we breathe. Yes, I have faith, and I wish every one of you did as well.

Yesterday I saw a sight which I have never seen in my lifetime and frankly it frightened me a little. Why because it got me to wondering. I saw a single white bird among the great mass of the gathering birds. Was this a sign from above? Or it might have been an albino or some other freak of nature? I couldn't say one way or another. I read lots of books concerning end times, so maybe my mind just got carried away. You see I was sitting in one of my deer blinds reading a book. It was approaching dusk. The gathering birds out near our large pond were getting noisy. My guess is that the birds were possibly discussing all aspects of their upcoming trip south. The ground was alive with hundreds of very loud birds. A couple weeks ago I broadcast rye seed and dragged it. This left thousands of rye kernels on top of the ground. The gathering birds used their skills to locate the uncovered seeds knowing they needed the strength to be able to endure the long, difficult journey ahead. If you ask people how the birds know what to do they say, instinct. But how are animals able to pass along information needed for their very survival from generation to generation if birds are not considered that smart? Do you and I need to prepare for a trip ahead as well? None of us know the time when we will leave this place. The white bird got my attention. So tell me if you have ever seen a white blackbird in your lifetime?

Let it Snow

The snow is really rolling in this fall, isn't it? It doesn't seem to help anything if I complain so I'll skip that part. Actually, I love to sit in a nice spot and watch it snow. My deer blind is my favorite place to watch the snow for the past couple weeks but yesterday ended that as firearms deer season ended. Now I relax and watch our very lively bird feeders and make soup. Warm bread would be especially good with my soup so I best stop loafing and get busy. I was looking for a way to get some exercise today so I left my tractors parked and got out the snow blower. It worked great, I sweated up a storm, right in the midst of the blowing snow storm.

The highway guys and gals at the DOT are probably pretty happy about now. This storm will likely get them a bit of overtime Christmas money. The Marion Village workers were out blowing snow up and down Main Street this morning- they actually looked happy. We guys like to use those big toys I believe. I was out 4 wheeling in my pick-up truck today checking out the country roads and seeing if the big buck deer I had hoped to shoot was out moving about. No sign of them out my way.

Soups on and I finally got out the Betty Crocker's Best Bread Machine Cookbook. My wife will be glad to get home and smell what I have been up to today. During deer season I had been slacking off on cooking good meals. Turkey noodle soup from our leftovers for tomorrow sounds tasty.

The weather man might be sending me outside again before long, it's piling up again. Oh my, the life as a retired teacher is such a wonderful blessing. I did give thanks, several time last week for the privileges I have. Bring on that snow although my calendar seems to be a little off kilter is it winter already on December first?

The Man from the Woods

Don Spoor was quite a guy. Unfortunately, he recently drown while swimming in the Manistee River. He was only thirty-three years old and the father of four children in the prime of his life. I spoke briefly at his funeral this last Thursday. I told the huge funeral crowd of around five hundred, how much I enjoyed having him as a student in my class as well as his sister, Jesse. Don was character but a good character! He was a very highly skilled sawyer and woodsman even as a teenager. Don actually helped me teach other students the finer points of felling trees and safely using a chainsaw. His efforts helped our FFA Chapter to receive a National FFA Safety award. We got the award at the National Convention in Kansas City, Missouri. I was his instructor at the Wexford- Missaukee Area Career Technical Center in Cadillac. He received the State FFA Degree while there as a student; which is the highest award given in the state. Don was also a member of our school's National FFA Forestry Contest Team where they competed representing Michigan and received a Bronze medal at Nationals. Having enjoyable students like Don made the sometimes difficult and stressful job of working with students where people can die in the woods all worth it.

Donny actually listened to me as a student. The sayings I passed along to the students over the years- ones like, "help other people as best you can, or there is no limit to what you can accomplish if you don't care who gets the credit!" Don took the next step and made the saying come alive by using and applying them in kind and loving ways. The Bible says to love your neighbor as yourself, applying the living word is the best way to honor God.

Several people thanked me for being his teacher and for speaking at the funeral. I told them all the same thing, "That it was my privilege to know him and be his teacher." Don's mother lovingly summed up who her son was saying, "Don worked hard, played hard and loved hard!" You do not get that many people at your funeral unless you're a special person. Some of his friends, several who were also my students, spoke at the funeral as well. Each shared stories like how Don would drive for hours just so he could eat supper with his wife and family. He would do that even when he had worked hard all day in the woods as far away as the Big Mac Bridge. One young guy told me how Don learned how some old people near where they were logging last winter were out of heating wood. Don went and asked the owners of the land if he and his crew could cut up some tops for the old couple. The owner's agreed with his plan, so they cut, split, delivered, and stacked the wood to the then tearful couple- people they didn't even know. People shared many other stories of Don's kindness of a similar nature. More than two hundred cars journeyed to the cemetery, and people did not want to leave even after the service had ended. The funeral director finally asked people to leave so the family could have a few quiet moments alone. Don's mother told me her daughter knew I would come. It was a difficult day, but it was the right thing to do. God ways are difficult to understand at times. This again was a case then my role was determined from above well before this day. People were choked up during the funeral, so then people were asked to say a few words no one went forward. So I went up first and got the ball going, and several others then followed. This is the fifth time God has called upon me to go first at a funeral. I will be lucky to have fifty people at my funeral but five hundred wow. Don Spoor was a regular guy that did simple good deeds for others, and people loved and respected him for it. May God's peace be with you all. P.S. When you think of Don I suggest you watch the movie, "The Man from Snowy River" you'll see why when you view it.

Quaking Aspen and Whispering Pines

The sounds of the wind through the trees often create a calm and peaceful feeling. Most men and women living in our computer age fail to set aside the time to hear the revitalizing beat of mother earth. I was given a very rare gift from above today. God and new construction on M-115 in front of our house combined to grant me a special and unexpected treat. Silence and no noise from traffic for periods of up to five minutes at a time. I was sitting on a lawn chair out at the end of my driveway watching the grind-off and repaving project. Then things got going it was more like a full blown circus. Dozens of trucks both dump and asphalt, graders, rollers, power sweepers, grinders, paving machines, pickups galore, traffic directors and more. At times in the midst of all this activity, I could actually hear the Aspen leaves quaking or twisting back and forth rapidly in the brisk breeze. The Spruce trees seemed to whisper my name and said, "Be still my friend!" It was a different sound than that of the wispy talk of the great white pine. Cars speed past my house very rapidly under normal circumstances but not Monday with the all the highway work in progress. Traffic was slowed to a crawl giving people time to see someone like me near the road. It must be rare to see someone relaxing out-of-doors in these present times. People waved and smiled non-stop as they did in times past for the entire afternoon. I watched the road repair show while marveling at the positive response the passersby graced me with. It somehow gave me the idea or notion that people may still long for a slower quieter life. Did they see me catching a brief moment of good-old neighborly fun and were wishing they could've joined me? Maybe I was only dreaming and wishing that we could, as necessary, reach up and turn back those clock hands a few turns. Do you find the time to enjoy the simple things of life when you're given a chance to see an event like I saw Monday? It cost me nothing, and I even napped a couple of times, as a guy at the ten o'clock coffee club pointed out to me today. I'll keep my story short because a couple of people said to me that when they look too long, they don't always read them. Have a lovely day and may peace be with you always.

The Blue Memory Fire

We each have our memories of the Johnson farm, of the hills overlooking the Kalamazoo River Valley. One special one is that of twin black sweet cherry trees. I am resting now watching the unique blue-green flames of those famous trees while recording a few happy, fun times we shared. I was asked to remove the crumbling limbs of those very cherry trees last summer. It sure is odd that forty years after enjoying the fruits I am now enjoying the light and heat by burning their wood.

The power is out this evening in Hagar Shores, very near Coloma, due to a winter wind storm. The results of the lovely quiet allow me to hear the crashing surf from the waves on Lake Michigan, about one-quarter mile away. The mild winter is causing severe problems. The normally iced up shoreline is totally exposed to the wind and waves.

The lights and TV are out. I suppose that's what slowed down time and pushed me back to other days of the past. The black cherry story started over 40 years earlier.

One warm June day the birds, especially our state bird, the bobbing robin, were active. The chirping and fussing were the signal that our cherries were starting to ripen. The trees were located just past the 160-foot long dairy cattle barn, along the lane.

It was such a warm, sunny day and my partner that day was Sox, a friendly standard collie. The dog looked like Lassie and myself like TV's Timmy. As we passed the black sweet-cherries, it struck me that my time to munch some would soon come along.

The cows were in the closest pasture, thus also being the easiest for rounding them up. We circled behind the cows, and they slowly began trudging toward the milking barn. They stirred up a bit of dust once we reached the lane. I never pushed the cows, my style was to let them drag along at a mild pace. Each cow ambled into the barn door, and each one used the same stanchion each day. Cows like a smooth return – like children or adults. I slid the door closed when I saw Dad had put their feed in front of each feeding cow. The stanchions were being clicked shut. Then a smile lit my face. I headed over for a few cherries.

My next task awaited, feeding the calves warm milk replacer. I had to go to the house for the hot water. I dreaded that part due to the weight. I was 65 – 70 pounds and the pails of hot water, 40 – 50 pounds. Spilling them was not an option as hot water cost money – something we had little of. You mixed in cups full of powdered milk and carried small pails to the dozen or so calves. You had to train each calf to drink by putting your arm into the pail and allowing the calves to suck your finger. You kept removing your fingers and in time, they drank it straight out of the pail. You were now wet and smelly.

A typical working day on the family farm had ended. The memory fire flickered and waved goodnight. May God's peace be with you, now and always.

A Special Note:

I am more of a storyteller than a writer or skilled author. All proceeds from the sale of this book at any of these locations will be donated to that organization or group:

1. The Michigan 4-H Foundation,
   http://www.mi4hfdtn.org
2. The Michigan FFA Foundation,
   http://www.michiganffa.com/foundation/Default.htm
3. Friends Ministry of Lake City and Marion
   http://www.friendsministry.net
4. Marion Public Library Book Fund,
   http://www.marion-library.org
5. Lake City CRC Youth Group,
   http://www.lakecitycrc.org/ministries/youth-ministries.cfm
6. Wexford-Missaukee Area CTC Scholarship Fund,
   http://www.wmisd.org/career-technical-education/ctc-scholarships

7. Michigan State University – Varsity S Club, http://msuvarsitysclub.org
8. Project Cane Fire – Missions Fund, http://www.projectcanefire.org
9. And others to be named …

During my developing years, I benefitted greatly from 4-H, FFA, Scouts and church participation. Donating this book at no cost to these groups is my attempt to pay back those organizations that now help others.

May God, Jesus Christ, and the Holy Spirit be with you now and forever.

Dale M. Johnson

:^)

Made in the USA
Middletown, DE
26 October 2016